774628

798.25   Green, Carol
Gre
         Jumping
       explained

JUMPING EXPLAINED

Overleaf: Brian Young riding Top Sawyer at Badminton 1953

CAROL GREEN

JUMPING EXPLAINED

A Horseman's Handbook

Arco Publishing Company, Inc.
New York

ALSO IN THE SERIES

DRESSAGE EXPLAINED
TRAINING EXPLAINED
STABLE MANAGEMENT EXPLAINED
SHOWING & RINGCRAFT EXPLAINED

Published in the U.S.A. by Arco Publishing Company, Inc.
219 Park Avenue South, New York, N.Y. 10003
by arrangement with Ward Lock Limited

© Midas Books 1976

First published in Great Britain in 1976
by Ward Lock Limited, 116 Baker Street, London W1M 2BB,
a member of the Pentos Group

Photography by R. N. Targett
Printed in Great Britain

Library of Congress Cataloging in Publication Data

Green, Carol.
    Jumping explained.

    1. Show jumping. I. Title.
SF295.5.G73 1976b   798′.25   76-26622
ISBN 0-668-04116-1
ISBN 0-668-04085-8 pbk.

CONTENTS

Acknowledgments

We are particularly indebted to Brian Young, FHBS, DBHS, Managing Director of Crabbet Park Equitation Centre, Worth, Sussex, (formerly National Instructor at The British Horse Society) and Miss Valerie Lee, BHSI, for help and advice in the preparation of this book; to Miss Marie Stokes, FBHS, Proprietress and Director of Equitation, Walton Heath Livery Stables, Tadworth, Surrey, for her great assistance and technical advice, also for allowing her horses and facilities at Walton Heath to be used for the photographs; to Mrs Hatton-Hall FBHS for all her kindness, help and encouragement throughout the years of my own training; to Bob Targett whose photographs have so enriched this publication and to the riders who made this book possible.

LIST OF ILLUSTRATIONS

LIST OF COLOUR ILLUSTRATIONS

LIST OF COLOUR ILLUSTRATIONS *(Continued)*

1 Choice of the horse for jumping

Good jumping horses come in many different shapes and sizes. The salient characteristics of successful horses, however, are courage, an instinct for self-preservation and a natural ability for jumping.

If you are on the point of purchasing a horse for show-jumping or for competing in sporting activities which come under the general equestrian heading of 'eventing', you must first look at his general appearance considering the good and bad features. As a novice trainer you will not have the wisdom to make your own choice and will naturally seek expert advice.

The horse should be pleasing to the eye and have what is called 'presence' which is to say personality coupled with vitality, and be nimble footed. The best results will be achieved by a horse showing quality, well proportioned and with an alert head.

In a quality horse one should see a small head, well 'set on' to the neck with a large, bold or generous eye. He should be short in the back, with the outline, from the neck along the back to the dock, a series of well-pleasing curves. He should have a deep girth indicating to the professional that there is plenty of room for the heart and lungs to function properly. The horse should have short, strong loins and plenty of length from the point of hip to the point of hock, i.e. well let down; he needs strong quarters, a muscular second thigh and tail well set on. The feet are naturally very important and should be of good shape with the forefeet rounded and the hindfeet slightly oval, consisting of good sound horn and a well-developed frog. The horse's legs should show plenty of bone in proportion to his overall frame. The amount of bone is the measurement around the foreleg just below the knee, 21.6 centimetres being good. The energy which will enable your horse to jump big fences comes from the hindquarters; therefore I consider the length of his back to be important. The length of back is an indication of this potential in that a horse with a long back can often have problems in collected work and may experience difficulty with combination fences where distances between the jumps are short. A horse possessing a short back, combined with strong quarters and well-rounded loins which allow for muscle development and hocks which are large, low and nicely 'bent', should prove a better 'buy'. The neck should be set well upon gradually sloping shoulders. When trotted in hand the horse's action should be free—with no trace of short, jarring strides.

Whatever the horse's breeding, he must have a calm temperament. The easily upset, highly strung horse will tend to be erratic in behaviour when jumping, and careless in movement across country. When looking at a horse with a view to buying him it is advisable, if you can, to see the horse lunged over a fence without a rider. In this way you will see whether he enjoys jumping or is reluctant, whether he rounds his back when jumping loose and gains momentum in his approach to a fence. If he 'gets under'—that is to say, delays his take-off at a jump—this may be an indication of his having been 'chased' over fences and forced to jump without proper preliminary schooling. Watch the horse for a well-developed timing of his own stride when he is jumping combination fences loose. Very often a horse that appears to jump well enough while ridden does not give such an impressive performance when loose. This can be because, when ridden over a fence, the horse has been supported too much by the rider's legs and hands and has not been called upon to use his own initiative and self-balance.

The good show-jumping horse must be consistently obedient to the rider's lightest aid, quick to respond to the rider's legs when jumping and on the flat. He should be trained in smooth manoeuvrability and in the following chapters I will endeavour to describe the best ways to achieve this and other accomplishments expected of the good show-jumping and cross-country horse.

2 The rider

The successful rider over fences must be dedicated to the sport and before aspirants attempt to develop style and jumping technique they should spend a considerable part of their time establishing a good seat. A finished rider should be a good all-round equestrian, possessing enthusiasm, patience and an easily asserted sense of humour. Impatience and ill-temper will quickly be conveyed from rider to horse—to the confusion of the latter and failure of both.

Those who aspire to show-jumping will have seen that the rider's seat is a forward one. Stirrups need to be shortened three to four inches from the length you have when riding on the flat. This enables the weight of the rider to be absorbed at the knee and into the stirrup irons, so that the angles in front of the hip, behind the knee and in front of the ankle are slightly more closed compared with a normal riding position on the flat. The rider will improve his seat by work over small grids and combination fences, developing what is known as an independent seat, which allows the horse to jump with ease, less hampered by the rider's weight.

In his approach to an obstacle the horse which jumps well lowers his head and stretches his neck in order to assess in advance the size of that obstacle and the precise point in his stride for take-off. The head and neck are the horse's main balancing points and when watching a horse jumping one can see the extension of neck and head right out in front before his forelegs leave the ground. This allows him to shorten and check his final strides and places him for his take-off. It is most important, therefore, that his rider maintains contact with his mouth in that approach, taking particular care that hands are relaxed and supple, following the movement of the horse's head. In this way any interference from the rider is kept to a minimum.

In the crucial take-off stride the horse will raise his neck and head just before raising his forehand, thus allowing the weight of his rider to be carried over his shoulders. In this pose the horse's shoulder joints are opened and give muscular force which raises the forehand in the first stages of the ascent. At this juncture the rider must maintain contact with the reins whilst allowing the horse complete freedom of his head and neck to retain his balance. The horse's neck is extended forwards and downwards as the forelegs are lifted to begin the jump, the head and neck helping to lift the shoulders and forelegs over the fence.

The hindlegs have here been well engaged forwards under the horse's body through the joints of the hind legs. The horse's moment of suspension begins as the hind feet leave the ground and, when the forelegs have cleared the jump, the head and neck are raised immediately from their previous forward and lowered positions. When the horse is actually in flight over the obstacle it is most important that his rider stays in balance with his seat clear of the saddle and maintains this position on the landing stride, because, if the rider sits in the saddle as the hind legs are clearing the fence, the horse is likely to flatten the line of his back, lower his hindquarters and thus hit the fence with a hind leg.

As the horse lands he uses his head and neck in such a way as to absorb the jarring to his forelegs, also to adjust his balance for the getaway stride. The successful rider must consider the whole movement of the horse in his jump to appreciate the need to develop a position which is supple, balanced and fluid and puts minimum pressure on the reins, so that the horse has freedom to carry out the movements described with as little interference as possible. If the rider can 'resist' gently with his hands whilst increasing pressure with his legs, the horse will remain calm and confident in that gentle control which exists between legs and hands. This will give the rider compressed energy which can be released as, and when, required.

In the moment of suspension the rider should be looking forwards in the direction of travel, with the lower leg encasing the horse's 'barrel' and the arms coming well forward with a bend at the elbows to allow sufficient rein for the horse to take his first strides in the resumed canter after landing. The rider should then become more upright, taking up the reins and re-establishing normal feel in the hand in preparation for the approach to the next obstacle.

The jumping of grids and combination fences will assist the rider to develop a balanced and supple seat and achieve harmony of movement with his horse.

The foregoing are guilde-lines to the skill expected of a competition rider and the strict application of them will demand infinite patience and determination.

Master Pepe with a young rider competing in the Pony Club Horse Trial Championships at Stoneleigh. The Pony Club Horse Trials are an excellent training ground for both the young rider and the novice horse.

3 Principles of training on the flat

In order to increase the athletic ability and obedience of the horse it is necessary to know the various schooling movements and agility exercises used in the basic training of a young horse on the flat. Such movements develop the horse's response to the leg aids, an essential to the show-jumping horse.

The usual turns and figures ridden in a school or *manège* are on a single track, changing the rein by turning down the centre or diagonally across the school and going to the opposite track, riding loops and circles, turns on the forehand, serpentines and changes of direction within the circle. All these movements should first be carried out at the walk—when horse and rider will find them easier to perform. A good size of *manège* to work in is 50 metres by 25 metres.

As the horse's balance improves, the rider should progress through to the trot, riding these movements at the faster pace, except for the turn on the forehand which should be performed from the halt. The horse should look in the direction he is moving, bent from his poll to his dock around the rider's leg; so by working him with plenty of changes of direction your intention to render him more responsive to aids will be realised. A horse may lose impulsion, or energy, on turns and this must be anticipated by riding energetically and firmly forwards so that the rhythm of the stride is not lost, maintaining impulsion from his rear and avoiding shortened steps on the turns.

Balance is most important to the horse whilst jumping for his centre of gravity is altering perpetually as he tackles different types of obstacles. The horse learns to balance himself before he is ridden, and when he is being ridden he must learn to be balanced with the rider. This is when his weight and that of the rider are distributed in such a way to allow him to move with maximum efficiency. As an untrained young horse, while grazing in a more or less natural state, he carries two thirds of his whole weight on his forehand but the trainer tries to encourage the horse to shift this weight towards the rear so that it is more evenly distributed over all four legs. When he is moving, the horse's centre of gravity is moving constantly; it is by the position of the horse's head and neck that his centre of

14

gravity moves forwards as the pace increases or becomes extended, and backwards as the pace decreases or becomes more collected.

From normal balance the trainer must progress to developing fluid balance—that is, shifting the horse's centre of gravity smoothly back and forth without any jolting of horse or rider. From this fluid balance rhythm in pace is achieved. Rhythm with necessary impulsion can be attained by trotting over cavalletti. Whether you are hoping to train a horse for events, show-jumping, or simply want a bold horse which will carry you well all day in the hunting field, do not attempt intensive schooling whilst he is very young. Ponies may begin formal training at three years as a pony tends to develop more quickly than a horse.

When the horse is three years old his training may begin. Do not attempt this without someone to help you who is experienced in training young horses. The programme to follow is outlined in *Training Explained*. This early training follows the same pattern whether your horse is destined to compete as an event horse, show-jumper, or dressage horse. Briefly, he will be lunged, taught to carry a rider, carry out simple exercises in the *manège*, hack out with an experienced horse for company, then be turned out for six months to continue growing. Bring him in during the spring when he is four years old and continue his training following the programme given in *Training Explained*.

You can develop a young horse's balance by a course of lungeing with him saddled up, teaching him to move on a circle, and working for smooth transitions without losing either rhythm of pace or impulsion.

From the lunge work go on to mounted work, both on a loose rein and on a contact. It is good training to ride the horse on a loose rein sometimes so that he does not come to depend entirely upon the rider's hands. Work over ground rails should begin at this point and then jumping small grids and combination fences, which accustoms the young horse to shift his balance quickly and increases suppleness. This last is an exercise which develops the muscles of the horse's back, loins and gaskins. It will also encourage the youngster to jump in good style.

In the physical and mental make-up of a successful show-jumping horse able to use initiative and 'take on' large obstacles at shows or on cross-country rides, we look for smooth, free forward movement, the horse progressing calmly, obediently and actively. It is most important, therefore, that he understands and answers to the aids at the slightest indication from his rider. By systematic and regular work it is possible to develop the young horse's natural paces so that he will perform the job which is asked of him with keenness and courage, without losing calmness.

Never allow a horse to become bored or stale. He must have variety in his training work which should be both inside and outside the school. Give him plenty of work, using loops and serpentines to develop his lateral suppleness. Lunge him two or three times a week, using changes of pace to make his back more supple. The training on the flat of a young jumping horse should be brought to the level of the novice dressage horse.

Show-jumping courses are becoming more complicated in design, so take time and trouble to train your horse well in simple dressage so that he moves smoothly and responds immediately to your controlling aids.

A young horse in a Foxhunter competition at Hickstead. Notice that the rider is looking with head forward for the next fence.

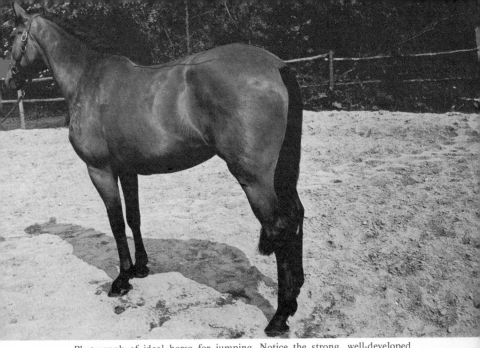

Photograph of ideal horse for jumping. Notice the strong, well-developed hindquarter

The rider showing classical jumping position

Lunge work will develop the horse's natural balance

Work on a loose rein over ground rails encourages the horse to lower his head and neck

Jumping a fence on the lunge rein

Notice the use of a surcingle over the forward-cut jumping saddle

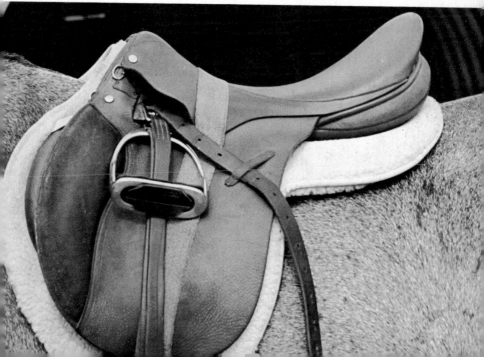

Trotting poles. Notice the horse's protective clothing of brushing boots and over-reach boots

Three ground rails to a small fence 3.25 metres away; this is a good way of introducing the young horse to jumping

4 Application of the aids

The means of communication between rider and horse are the natural and the artificial aids. The former are rider's body seat, legs, hands and voice, whilst the latter include whips, spurs, martingales and running reins.

It is important that the young horse learns to respond instantly to the rider's aids — training him first on the flat, and later over small fences. The horse will ultimately develop sufficient confidence in his rider to respond instantly and will go where the rider intends him to go. Throughout the training the rider demonstrates what he requires of the horse by the association of ideas. A simple example is seen in the grooming, when a trainer presses his hand to the side of the horse with the word 'over'. The horse gradually associates the word with the touch of his trainer's hand and will learn to move over. When a horse shows that he understands a newly-taught aid he should be rewarded with a pat and a kindly spoken word.

In show-jumping the means of communication are, of course, by touch — with the horse's reaction to seat, legs and hands. The driving or 'pushing' aids are applied by the rider's body and seat through the bracing of his back muscles, the legs by closing the insides of the calves of the legs against the horse's sides, and the hands by guiding the horse and regulating the energy created by the rider's seat and legs. The voice, spurs and whip may be needed, at times, as supplementary aids. The slowing down or 'stop' aids are the straightening of the rider's back whilst closing the legs inwards and feeling gently on the reins. The successful rider must develop a 'feel' for the horse's movement and be able to anticipate any evasion on the horse's part which he will counteract by use of legs in conjunction with reins. By practice the rider develops such co-ordination that he can use legs and hands independently of each other. When jumping, loss of balance on the part of the rider may cause the horse to collect penalties either by refusing or by knocking down the fence.

To handle the reins well with a minimum of interference with the horse's performance is only achieved if a rider continually improves the depth of his seat. You will have heard the equestrian expression 'good hands' applied to a rider — this indicates that the rider's hands are sympathetic but effective in giving signals to the horse for precision and control without losing the depth of his seat.

The simple aids are used diagonally. For example, to turn the horse to the right the rider should look to the right, placing the right leg at the girth with the left leg behind the girth feeling with the right rein so that the horse is looking to the right; the left rein, however, relaxing sufficiently to allow the horse to go to the right, without losing contact. When making any turn or change of direction it is important for the rider to look in the desired direction so that his weight instinctively tends that way. This will make it easier for the horse to answer the aid.

When jumping a course of fences it is to be presumed that the rider will be looking in his direction of travel (staring at the ground or looking only immediately in front of the horse is bad practice) whilst keeping proper control and sitting well; he should be anticipating the size and nature of jumps to be taken and this will necessitate looking ahead.

The rider who continues to look forwards in the direction of travel will find that the horse will land over a fence in a balanced canter stride and, more important, he will most probably be cantering with the desired leg leading and able to make more economical turns, thereby saving time in a competition 'against the clock'.

A transition is the change from one pace to another; for example, from walk to trot, trot to canter, canter to trot, trot to walk, or within a pace by lengthening or shortening the stride.

A transition should be carried out smoothly with the horse maintaining regularity of stride up to, and following, the transition. The secret of a good transition is to prepare yourself and the horse for the change by thinking in terms of 'I have time' and in that time—think! The rider must sit still and upright in the saddle, close both legs inwards, resist a little with the hands but as he feels the horse 'give', lighten the hand and ride him forwards. The rider may find that in a downwards transition from trot to walk the horse loses impulsion. This is because, having used aids for the downwards transition, the rider was not quick enough to recover and lighten the hand, nor to use the legs to send the horse energetically forward. Transitions are important, both at the slow and faster paces, and it is well worth while practising until horse and rider are able to carry them out precisely.

If your own and your horse's training has been thorough and undertaken on correct principles you should have no difficulty in combined training competitions (dressage with jumping), show-jumping or horse trials (dressage, show-jumping and cross country).

The show-jumping horse must be trained to respond instantly to the rider's lightest aids since he will be required to cope with big fences—some of intricate design, within a time limit—at speed. If your sights are set upon horse trials, then it will not be sufficient simply to train your horse to jump. He will need to be as bold and accurate as any show-jumper but will also have to be sufficiently well-trained to take dressage tests and have reached a greater degree of fitness for fast work as well as being able to jump a great variety of natural-looking obstacles at speed.

The author riding her own horse Limelight at Crookham Horse Trials. Notice the good position of the rider.

5 Development of a horse's natural jumping ability

In the training of a young horse it is important to realise that whilst his body must be hardened, his muscles must be made strong but also supple.

Work over ground rails is an exercise in which the horse is able to use his muscles and loosen his back, encouraging the lowering of the head and improving his suppleness.

If this basic training is correctly carried out over a period of several months, it will stand the young horse in good stead in all his future competitive work.

The horse must proceed in a smooth movement and in complete harmony with its rider. The rider who works too hard will destroy impulsion and the rhythm he is trying to achieve. It is important that the rider takes time and trouble to establish an independent seat which is relaxed—without tension though still readily active.

It is best to begin work on a loose rein. In this way the trainee horse's neck will become independent of very close control and the horse will be able to adjust its own balance. The confident, free-going horse will not run away but go with a 'round' back which is supple. When the horse moves calmly on a loose rein it is a good idea to re-establish rein contact and work him from behind, encouraging him to 'take the rider's hand' and thus seeking his own contact with the bit while he is ridden in large loops and circles. Practise lengthening and shortening the stride when working around small fences. Test the regularity of the trot by working the horse over ground rails which are placed 1.40 metres apart. In all this work the horse must be urged forwards so that energy comes from the hind legs.

The spine of the horse has little lateral flexion with a very mobile 'forehand'. It is the ability of the horse to flex his hind legs, to round his back and to lower his croup which enables him to be light in his forehand and supple in the work described here. Work on the circle will increase lateral flexion of the spine while transitions will develop longitudinal suppleness of the back. Work over ground rails or cavalletti helps to keep the young horse's mind alert. With the young horse it is best to begin with three poles on the ground (ground rails). First urge the horse to begin his work at a good, regularly paced walk with the rider maintaining the lightest possible rein contact — not held by the rider's grip on the reins but allowed to establish his own stride. When the horse is walking over the rails confidently he should be urged to trot over them — still with a light rein contact. Ground rails are used at this point because to work a very young horse at the trot over raised poles or cavalletti is dangerous and risks overstraining the joints of his legs. The poles should be 1.40 metres apart to begin with when working a horse of approximately 15 hands. (See Diagram 1).

In these early lessons your aim is to win the confidence of your horse. Encourage the horse to enjoy jumping and to develop confidence in his own ability, whilst establishing a good style.

A young horse should not be 'overfaced' — that is to say, he should not be urged to jump obstacles which are too big for him so early in his career. Place ground rails and small fences in such a way that they will encourage the trainee to jump them with ease. Try to arrange as many variations as possible, using a placing rail to assist the horse in finding his way to any small fence effortlessly and confidently, knowing where he should come to his take-off stride. This elementary gymnastic jumping will inspire that self-confidence mentioned above.

A simple arrangement is to put the placing rail 50 centimetres high about 5.50 metres before a small obstacle approximately 80 centimetres high. The horse and rider approach in trot, trot over the first element, continue in canter and then jump the 80 centimetres obstacle (see Diagram 2). Various trot and canter exercises can be built around this arrangement.

Diagram 1

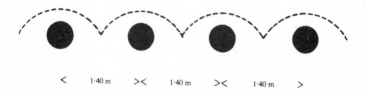

<   1·40 m   ><   1·40 m   ><   1·40 m   >

Footnote   15 hands = 152.5 cms.

Diagram 2

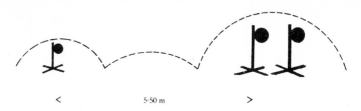

<   5·50 m   >

Make these simple jumping arrangements as varied as possible so that the horse, in repeating the same exercise, does not begin to anticipate exactly what is going to be asked of him and therefore to start to 'rush his fences'. This will defeat the training object and the horse will become uninspired in his work — jumping 'flat'. If the horse should tend to become excited, work him around a number of obstacles without jumping them and calm him before resuming jumping again.

Hill work is worthwhile as an exercise and is an essential part of the horse's physical fitness programme, improving his respiration and strengthening the appropriate muscles and tendons.

Prix Caprilli competitions are a good introduction to competitive riding for both the horse and the novice rider.

6 Loose-schooling and jumping exercises

Before work commences over ground rails, cavalletti or small fences, the horse must be accustomed to wearing the appropriate protective equipment. For his work over the cavalletti the horse wears brushing boots on all four legs and a pair of over-reach boots on the forelegs — lack of confidence can result from the horse striking himself accidentally.

When the young horse appears to be self-confident and accustomed to the rider-trainer's voice, loose-schooling may begin.

Oddly enough, 'loose-schooling' must be carried out in an enclosed space — a well-fenced *manège* or indoor school. The indoor school should not be too large — approximately 20 x 30 metres. If a school is too large it is so much more difficult for the trainer closely to control the horse. The same principles apply here as for lungeing, in that the trainer stays level with the horse's girth.

The horse is sent on a circle around the trainer in the same way **as when lungeing on a large circle. As the horse becomes more** obedient to the voice, he may be kept to the outer track of the *manège*. During this part of his training the horse must not be fussed or hustled but must proceed calmly in response to voice and whip. If the horse is allowed to become apprehensive of the trainer he will become prone to rush his fences when the time comes and will hollow his back and jump badly.

Loose jumping helps to develop the necessary muscles and encourage the horse to use full freedom of his head whilst at the same time allowing for the rounding of his back and the required folding of his legs for the jump.

A good arrangement for loose-school jumping is to have two fences, the first an upright followed by a parallel 6.50 metres away; both fences to be approximately 0.75 metres high (see below).

Diagram 3

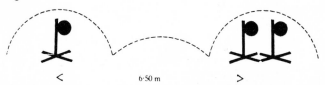

<   6·50 m   >

Combination jumps keep the horse mentally alert. The upright jump to a spread will encourage the horse to use his shoulders and will lighten his forehand at the first element. The comfortable distance of 6.50 metres to a spread will allow the horse to stretch out and jump in good style over the spread.

A cavalletto is a small jump with cross-legs at each end, enabling the jump to have three heights. Do *not* build up cavalletti to construct a higher jump. Horses have suffered serious injury by this make-shift arrangement. A horse can fall and hit such a fence, the elements of which do not easily separate, and create a dangerous tangle. When used as they should be, in conjunction with rails and stands for agility **exercises, cavalletti must still be used with great caution.**

Cavalletti work can develop the horse's jumping outline but should not be undertaken until the trainer is sure that the horse is obedient to the rider on the flat and has been loose-schooled or lunged over small fences.

Walk the horse over ground rails which are evenly spaced at about 1.40 metres apart. As the horse gains confidence he may be worked at the trot over these spaced rails. When he is working smoothly at the trot over ground rails — on a straight line and also in a circle — then he may be worked over the **cavalletti. Begin with three cavalletti** *at their lowest height* **at about 1.40 metres apart, trot a large circle of 20 metres diameter, then progress by going large from the well-shaped circle allowing the horse to stretch his neck while maintaining the lightest possible contact and retaining harmony between rider and mount.**

Diagram 4

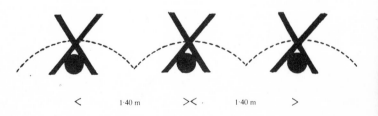

| < | 1·40 m | >< · | 1·40 m | > |

When the horse is working confidently over the three cavalletti — increase the number to four then five and trot over these without losing the regularity of the pace. Progressing from the work over ground rails and the trotting over cavalletti, the horse may be encouraged to jump a small fence. Place three cavalletti 1.40 metres apart at their lowest height and place a full-height cavalletti 2.80 metres away from the last. The rider should look forwards beyond the last cavalletto and the horse be urged to trot over the first three, maintaining regular pace, and jump the last element. Practise this exercise, sometimes going over the obstacles, sometimes riding large circles. By varying the exercise in this way the horse will not anticipate and 'rush his fences'.

Diagram 5

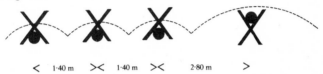

The horse must not be made to progress to canter work until the trot work is an established part of his training so far.
Progressing to canter exercises, begin again with ground rails set at 6.50 metres apart. The horse should take one canter stride over each rail with one stride in between — three poles being the maximum at this first stage. When the horse can go at an unhurried canter over the ground rails, they may be reduced to a distance of 3.25 metres apart.

Diagram 6

Diagram 7

Cavalletti work at the canter may be introduced when the ground rail cantering can be maintained at a regular stride and in an unhurried manner.

Place three cavalletti with 6.50 metres between each. Approach the exercise with an energetic canter but well controlled, riding to the centre of each cavalletto, with a feeling for increased impulsion as the horse starts to work down the grid.

Diagram 8

The horse should continue with this work in conjunction with the trot exercises until he is confident and able to jump cavalletti from trot or canter at the demands of his rider. More advanced work may be introduced by varying the distance of the canter cavalletti to 3 and 6.50 metres, making a little spread fence at the end of the course (Diagram 9). As the horse continues to improve, working on the circle with ground rails and cavalletti may be introduced, firstly at trot and then at canter.

Diagram 9

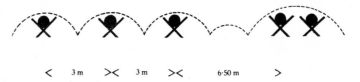

All the exercises using ground rails may now be carried out with cavalletti at their lowest height replacing the rails on the ground. Remember that, throughout his jumping, unless there is a good reason for not doing so, each fence should be approached on a straight line, to the centre of the fence and at right angles to it with a feeling for increased impulsion.

30

7 To summarise

In the foregoing suggested training programme I have assumed that the horse under training will be getting a minimum of one hour's work each day or six schooling sessions a week with a rest on the seventh day. A typical week should be spent as follows:

1st day—Your horse may well be fresh after his rest day so for the first ten to fifteen minutes you should work him on the lunge at walk, trot and canter, encouraging him to move calmly in all paces. In such work you should concentrate on his establishing a regular pace with smooth transitions from one pace to another.

When the horse is moving well on the lunge, then ride him. Begin at the walk and progress to trotting, introducing changes of direction, loops, serpentines, large circles and transitions. The rider-trainer should be aware of the horse's movements — of his rhythm in stride and feeling for that forward thrust of his power coming from his hindquarters. After about forty minutes, hack out for half an hour away from the school to give the horse variety so that he does not become stale in his work.

2nd day—In ridden work, begin by using wide loops and circles as on the first day — concentrating now on the correct bend while making frequent changes of direction. Finish this day's lesson by working the horse at a walk — first over one ground rail and progressing to three at 1.40 metres apart. The rider should sit still, maintaining only a light contact with the horse's mouth, allowing him to look at the ground and make his own judgement as to pace, so long as it remains unhurried.

3rd day—Commence again with ridden work — again in large loops and circles. The horse should at this point be urged to lengthen and shorten his stride when indicated by the rider. This helps him to adjust his equilibrium and lightens his forehand. Work on transitions from walk to trot, trot to canter, canter to trot, and trot to walk, always riding the horse on as straight a course as possible. After this work on the flat, lasting about half an hour, begin

31

work over ground rails — at walk and trot for about ten minutes — and then, if time allows, hack the horse out gently for half an hour.

4th day—Start today with fifteen minutes of lungeing and then go on to ridden work beginning with ground rails — at walk and then at trot with the poles set on the ground at 1.40 metres apart — to a small fence 2.80 metres from the last pole. The fence should not exceed 60 centimetres in height or 75 centimetres in width. If the horse works calmly at this exercise, work him on both a long and then a loose rein to help in his independence of movement.

A long rein is when the rider maintains a light contact with the horse's mouth whilst allowing him to stretch his head and neck forwards and down, and a loose rein is when the rider relinquishes all contact with the horse's mouth.

5th day—Work on the flat to develop the horse's response to the aids by using turns on the forehand, transitions from one pace to another — loops, circles and large serpentines. Go on to agility exercises over rails on the ground then to a small fence (see previous examples). If the horse works well, hack out for half an hour.

6th day—Begin work on the lunge. In the school build obstacles for three different agility exercises. The first should be a line of ground rails 1.40 metres apart — these for trotting over. Second exercise is planned with ground rails to a small fence; the third with a fence at a canter distance of 6.75 metres giving the horse one non-jumping stride between the two fences. Work on circles and changes of direction. Make use of all three exercises by occasionally trotting over the rails — sometimes over the ground rails and trot fence—then progress on to the canter exercise. Such a variety of movement and exercises will prevent the horse from anticipating too much. By switching from the flat to the jumping and then from jumping to the flat exercises, you will also ensure that he does not become over-excited.

7th day—Rest day for horse and rider — lead him out in hand or turn him into the field for two hours.

Hunter Trials are a good introduction to cross-country phase of a B.H.S. Horse Trial. The author riding a young horse over a stone wall at Maidstone and District Hunter Trials.

8 Types of jumps

Work over combination jumps is one of the best ways to develop the horse's judgement of stride and his agility between and over jumps. Work regularly over small jumps — work progressively by using low and varied combination jumps. At this stage, it is better to increase the spread of a jump rather than its height. The horse will learn to jump a jump smoothly and the exercise develops confidence in both rider and horse. The rider will benefit by strengthening his seat and feeling more secure in the saddle. When setting up combination jumps for training purposes it should be remembered that an upright jump will encourage a horse to lift his shoulders—this is not so important to the short-striding horse—while spread jumps encourage him to stretch out and to round his back. Careful planning of jumps for use at the trot and the canter, using uprights and spreads, assist the horse to jump with increasing skill and to continue to move in correct style. In the following pages you will see suggested lay-outs for training obstacles which can be arranged on your home-ground.

The first exercise, illustrated in Diagram 10, will help the horse to use his shoulders correctly with rounded back and balanced stride. Lay a ground rail 6.70 metres from a small upright jump 76 centimetres high. Place another ground rail 6.70 metres from the upright. Beyond the second ground rail erect a small spread jump 76 centimetres high by 90 centimetres wide and 7 metres from the last ground rail. The first ground rail, used for the non-jumping stride, will help the horse to correct his canter stride; the little upright, at the short distance of 7 metres, will help him to lighten his forehand and jump with accuracy—using thrust from his hindquarters. The second ground rail will again check the canter and ensure that the horse meets the spread jump well.

Diagram 10

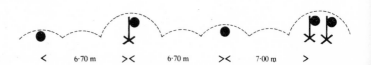

<   6·70 m   ><   6·70 m   ><   7·00 m   >

34

If the trainee-jumper proves to be impetuous, the rails on the circle, as indicated in Diagram 11, will help to prevent him from rushing at a jump. It is advisable to have such ground rails at a trotting distance in one part of the school away from that equipment used for the main exercises. By this arrangement it is possible to make variations in the curriculum of the horse's training by working around the jumps and then going over to the ground-rail work to check the regularity of the trot. A young and eager horse will feel more excited with his jumping exercises and the ground rails can be used occasionally to calm him before resuming his jumping again.

Diagram 11

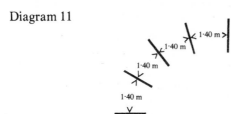

Distance between centre of 2 poles is 1.40 metres

Before going on to the remaining exercises it is necessary to do a certain amount of preliminary work over ground rails and cavalletti. Ground rails set in a curving course with ground rails to a trot jump as in Diagram 12, is a good exercise for the young horse which tends to become unbalanced.

Diagram 12

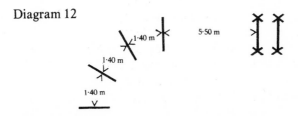

Distance between centre of 2 poles is 1.40 metres

The ground rails set on a circle will encourage extra thrust from the inside hind leg. The horse which has a tendency to run in the trot will develop a more positive and well-paced trotting stride. The action of coming out of a corner or out of a circle to progress then on a straight line, still using ground rails, and finishing with a spread fence about 5.50 metres from the last rail will train a horse to jump in good style, to land in a balanced manner and therefore to improve his departure from the fence.

If a young horse, when introduced to new jumps, is inclined to rush at them and show excitement, use the jump arrangement shown in Diagram 13.

Set up the four jumps so that each may be jumped from either direction; suggested jumps—brush, parallel bars, wall, planks; each one about 80 centimetres high. With this arrangement it will be possible to 'go round' taking each jump individually, or as a combination, or pass between them without any jumping, thus encouraging the horse to move according to your aids without rushing so that he cannot anticipate the rider's requirements.

Diagram 13

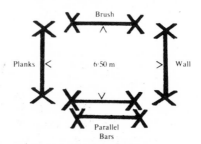

An exercise which should improve the horse's response to the rider's aids and control requires a total of twelve jump stands and ten poles. It is unlikely that you will have such facilities at home and so this should be carried out in a riding school which has adequate equipment. Diagram 14 shows the arrangement.

On a straight line set four ground rails at 1.25 to 1.50 metres apart, to within 3 metres of a small spread jump. Beyond the jump at a distance of 6.75 metres, place a second jump. Arrange an upright jump and another spread jump which can be jumped from both sides as shown. Riding this simple course is an excellent exercise for the horse, encouraging correct jumping from both trot and canter. The approach to each

Three small fences at a canter distance of 6.5 metres giving one non-jumping stride between each fence

Agility exercise of two rails to a small fence at a distance of 6.5 metres. The rails are raised to encourage the horse to jump

Work over ground rails at 1.40 metres apart on the 20-metre circle

Pole, upright fence, pole, to a spread fence, arranged at a distance of 6.5 metres in between each to ensure that the horse jumps with a round back

An upright fence to a spread fence at a short distance of 6.5 metres to make the horse jump from his hocks

Jumping a parallel fence to an upright at a distance of 8 metres

A parallel fence that can be jumped from both sides

A parallel fence that can be jumped obliquely to assist the horse in finding his take-off stride. Notice the line of approach the rider is taking

jump is important and the rider must make accurate turns and look forward to the next jump all the time.

Diagram 14

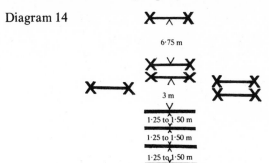

None of the exercises suggested here should be ridden more than two or three times during a training session and if at any stage in his training the performance of the horse suggests that he is becoming bored or stale or begins to refuse his jumps—or even run out—the trainer should revert to ground-rail work before resuming such formal training as described here.

Diagram 15 illustrates an exercise to be jumped from canter. It is a more advanced exercise than the previous one and should not be attempted until the horse is jumping adequately from the trot.

It should be noted that in Diagram 15 I have shown a combination jump of an upright to a spread at a fairly short distance—this is to train the horse to jump from his hocks. I have also shown two more simple jumps which the horse should be ridden to negotiate on completion of the double. The test of this canter exercise is whether or not the horse is able to come through the turns in canter, maintaining pace after successfully jumping the two jumps on a straight line.

Diagram 15

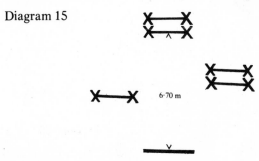

9 A four-week training programme for the novice show-jumper

So far we have dealt with the primary schooling and dressage training of the trainee jumping horse. If the horse has been properly trained in those basic stages, is responsive to the aids and moves well, more intensive and formal training can begin. The following day-by-day exercises should prepare the horse for entry into his first competitions.

First week

Monday—A rest day, lead the horse out 'in hand' for grass or turn him into his field.

Tuesday—Begin work in the *manège* using loops and circles and then progress to ground rails in trot to a little fence. The rider should canter in a forward position for jumping and practise lengthening and shortening the stride. Work on the exercise shown in Diagram 13, using the four jumps to form a 'box' and so discouraging the horse from rushing by alternating the jumping of one or more jumps and simply 'passing through' them. This exercise should last approximately five minutes. Then walk the horse on a long rein for about five minutes before returning him to his stable.

Wednesday—Work at transitions, circles and loops, then arrange the ground rails as shown in Diagram 12 to train the horse to establish rhythm in the trot. Next use jumps as shown in Diagram 14, urging the horse to jump an upright jump, then a spread firstly from the trot and then from the canter.

Work for half an hour before hacking out for half an hour.

Thursday—Lunge the horse for about fifteen minutes and then ride him for half to three-quarters of an hour in simple dressage exercises, changing the rein frequently.

Friday—Work at simple dressage exercises for forty minutes making transitions of pace. Set up a jumping exercise—a small jump, set 60 centimetres high at 5.50 metres from a small spread jump which is 90 centimetres high by 90 centimetres wide. Jump the first jump from trot and the horse should land, take one canter stride and jump the second jump. Jump this two or three times, then walk for five minutes on a long rein, dismount and return the horse to his stable.

Saturday—Hack across country carrying out exercises on slopes and hills if possible. If you encounter any logs or the trunks of fallen trees, provided they are of a suitable height, jump them to give the horse confidence working outside the *manège*.

Sunday—The horse may be exercised over a small course of jumps no higher than 76 centimetres. Work at both trot and canter.

Second week

Monday—Rest day.

Tuesday—Commence with gymnastic work and with ground rails arranged on a circular course. Then hack out for forty minutes.

Wednesday—Work on the flat including transitions and changes of direction.

Thursday—'Work in' for fifteen to twenty minutes. That is to say, exercise the horse in preparation for what follows— jumping exercises. These are best arranged to include a one non-jumping stride double (Diagram 16) and an in-and-out without a stride (Diagram 17).

Diagram 16

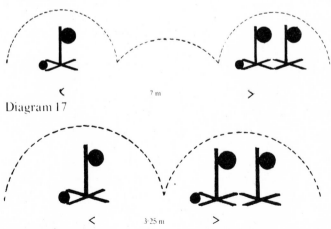

Diagram 17

7 m

3·25 m

Friday—This should be a day of simple dressage exercises similar to work on Wednesday. These exercises are important if the horse is to have the obedience of a really good show-jumper.

Saturday—Loose school the horse to develop his ability to adjust his take-off stride. Use upright and spread fences no higher than 90 centimetres. Such low obstacles will increase his confidence.

Sunday—Take the horse out for some cross-country jumping if this is available. If not, try to simulate a simple, small show-jumping course but restrict all jumps to a maximum of 90 centimetres and, if calmness is lost, circle in front of the jumps that you intend to jump.

Third Week

Monday—Rest day. Lead the horse out for grass or turn into his field.

Tuesday—First, use limbering-up exercises—'work in' the horse, after his rest day, with exercises at the trot on straight lines and on circles. Progress through to the canter maintaining the forward posture for jumping at all times. Jump two or three jumps from both canter and trot.

Wednesday—Practise some agility exercises already described and indicated in the diagrams. Make these a little more difficult by making the jumps a few centimetres wider and the distances between jumps a few centimetres longer (up to 7 centimetres), or a little shorter.

Thursday—Elementary schooling in dressage—using the whole area of the *manège* and making changes of speed and pace.

Friday—Work over combination jumps from canter and trotting exercises. Afterwards hack out for about thirty minutes.

Saturday—Limber-up in elementary training—transitions, turns, circles, lengthening and shortening stride. Work over ground rails and trot fences on a long rein to develop the horse's initiative whilst lightly controlled by the rider.

Sunday—Practise riding the horse over a simple course with emphasis on turns, taking care to spend time circling in front of jumps should the horse show signs of excitement.

Fourth week

Monday—Rest day.

Tuesday—Work the horse on a circle over ground rails and also on straight lines. Practise dressage training.

Wednesday—Arrange for one and a half hours of cross-country hacking.

Thursday—Lunge work over trot jumps to spreads using a parallel of up to 80 centimetres. Turn the horse out in his field to graze for an hour.

Friday—Practise agility exercises using both trot and canter distances. Progress to working on the circle using the parallel fence at 76 centimetres high.

Saturday—Hack across country and use hills and slopes if possible. Jump any small ditches encountered.

Sunday—Possibly this will be your first competition. By now your young horse should be established in basic training and jumping confidently. He should now be competent enough to be entered into a small local show, ready for a simple course. Do not expect to win on your first outing. The horse will be excited by the strange environment and may well be too strong for you to cope with him. If possible, the horse should have been taken previously to a show-ground without competing to get him accustomed to the strange sights and sounds. If you do enter, jump only one round, even if you are fortunate enough to have a successful round and 'go clear'. It would be a mistake to ride him 'against the clock' in a competition on his first appearance.

10 Hunting and Hunter Trials

Probably the best method of developing the courage and initiative of a young horse destined for show-jumping is to ride him in the hunting field. Before he is introduced to hunting, however, he should be thoroughly established in the primary training already described and completely obedient to his rider's aids otherwise there is a risk of spoiling his mouth. Care of the hunter follows in section 11.

Cub-hunting begins in September and the youngster may be taken about once a fortnight for up to two hours. Hunting also develops the horse's self-reliance in tackling unfamiliar obstacles in circumstances away from his home or school atmosphere. The foxhunting season begins early in November and, if you intend to go hunting, seek advice from someone experienced as it is a costly pastime and certain rules relating to manners and dress must be conformed to.

The fact that the horse is well-established in his elementary training and answers well to all aids makes it easier for the rider to observe common-sense precautions at the first meet. Keep the horse well under control—stay at the edge of the crowd. At the actual meet keep your horse facing the hounds. A young horse or pony will already feel excited by the atmosphere of other horses and people and may strike out at hounds which run behind him while he is standing. Ride round the edges of all fields planted with corn and do not gallop or jump unnecessarily. On the first few occasions do not stay out for more than about two hours. Dismount half a mile from your box or trailer, slacken off the girth and walk your horse back to the box or trailer. The horse will be tired after such exertion and should be rested next day, but he should be led out for twenty minutes to work off any stiffness.

In the hunting field the horse will encounter unfamiliar obstacles so it is best to accustom him to such jumps by jumping in company of others. Sometimes water presents a problem. Before taking a young horse over it for the first time, do make certain that the bed of that particular stream or wide ditch is sound. In all his training across country, even on quiet hacking, a young horse should have an older, more experienced horse ridden with him, to set an example when it comes to jumping obstacles and 'going through' water.

Hunter trials are another good method of introducing a young horse to cross-country work because the jumps are mostly natural obstacles and the course will be similar to the cross-country phase of a one-day event. Again, if you are going to compete in hunter trials ask someone knowledgeable to help you to make the entry for the competition and advise you as to the appropriate dress you will need to wear and the necessary equipment for your horse. Be sure that your horse's girths are secure and that all equipment fits well. A surcingle round your saddle is an extra safety precaution when jumping. I hope that your horse has been so well schooled that he is able to go across country in a snaffle with perhaps a running martingale fitted if he tends to become excited.

If you are entering for a hunter trial walk the course on foot at least twice, better still, three times. Keep the red flags on your right, white flags on your left. Other markers such as yellow arrows are direction markers only. You will have to pass between two markers to start and then again to finish and failure to do this will cause your elimination even if you have ridden a faultless round.

The first time you walk the course look for general points and walk the track you will actually ride. On the second walk round, look at each fence and decide how you intend to ride it—the approach, take-off and departure line. On the third walk round, look carefully at any fence or track which may not be straightforward.

When riding the course in the actual event, try to save your horse's energy by retaining your forward jumping posture, bearing on your knees. Do not go flat out uphill but try to conserve your horse's energy. Let your horse go at a faster pace downhill and on the flat where it is easier for him. At the end of the course when you have dismounted, slacken the girths, put an anti-sweat sheet over your horse and walk him in hand to cool and calm him. On your return to the horse-box look your horse over carefully for any cuts or abrasions he may have got on the ride over the course.

In such trials as these, it is a mistake for the novice to go too fast, risking refusals or a 'run out' because your horse is simply running away at speed without judgement. The canter pace is most important over such courses and a smooth, unhurried ride will add to both rider's and horse's confidence. Spring and autumn are the hunter trials' seasons. It is not unusual for the competitors to be judged in these for speed alone and it is the competitor who makes the fastest time cross-country without faults who wins. It is a mistake to hurry a young horse and therefore wise to treat these trials as *trials*, for your horse and yourself, as an intensive schooling exercise. Some of the cross-country competitions have 'pair' classes in which the class is judged on the performance of two riders and their mounts. This is an excellent opportunity for the young horse, which may have been prone to refuse, to regain confidence by following another, more experienced, horse; though sometimes in pairs they are required to go 'upsides', or alongside one another.

A junior rider jumping a spread fence at a local Horse Show.

11 Care of the young hunter-jumper

The day before hunting do not leave your horse in all day—he will be too fresh if it is his first season. Follow your usual routine as far as possible, with at least one hour of steady exercise involving half an hour's work on transitions and changes of direction, followed by half an hour's hacking. Check the horse's shoes to ensure that they are sound and in good condition with no risen clenches which occur when the points of the nails protruding from the hoof do not lie flush with the hoof but are raised. Groom him thoroughly. A horse which is to be hunted must be physically fit and free from any disorder, with no signs of cough or chill. When a horse has been introduced to hunting, he will come to anticipate the event with some rising excitement and therefore he should be late-fed regularly, or only after hunting. If he is not anticipating and is calm, give him a late-night feed on this, the day before the meet.

The day before the meet, check all your equipment for cleanliness and safety, especially the stitching. If you are travelling with a horse-box, ensure that you have bandages, rugs, tail guard, knee caps and over-reach boots ready, also hay for the return journey.

The day of the meet

1. Feed the horse two or three hours before leaving for the meet, adjusting the time for the length of the journey.
2. Allow the horse only very little hay beforehand—approximately 1 kilogramme. If the meet is at, say, 10.45 hrs, hay should have been eaten by 08.00 hrs. Give him the hay half an hour before you give him his hard feed.
3. Try not to break your regular routine or the horse which has been hunting may anticipate and go off his feed with excitement.
4. Groom him and then plait his mane.
5. 'Tack up' at least fifteen minutes before the horse is due to leave and thoroughly inspect.
6. If you are travelling by horse-box put a rug over the saddle, also put on the horse's head-collar over his bridle. Make sure the girths are slack. If the horse is saddled his back will

be warmed and he will be mounted so much more conveniently as soon as he is unloaded.

7. It is advisable to off-load about half a mile from the meet to allow you to hack to the meet while parking space is sought for the box by the driver. Many hunts ask that no boxes park within half a mile of the meet to avoid congestion.

Whilst the horse is away from his stable, or if you are alone before you leave for hunting, the stable should be prepared for the horse's return.

1. Put down a thick bed in the box.
2. Put 1.50-2.00 kilogrammes of hay well-shaken in a haynet, remembering to dampen the hay by tipping a bucket of water over the net to eliminate any dust in the hay, and hang up net outside the horse's stable.
3. Stand an empty water-bucket on one side.
4. Fold the rugs tidily in a corner of the box.

On the horse's return

1. Remove all tack except the saddle, unless the horse has remained saddled for more than half an hour in the trailer or box, in which case it may be removed and the back massaged. If hacked home, leave the saddle on for twenty minutes to half an hour but keep the horse tied up and put rugs on over the saddle. This is to allow the horse's circulation to return to normal after carrying the rider's weight for several hours.
2. A little luke-warm water may be given to the horse—half a bucketful—not cold water because it would be a shock to the system. Give him his hay and encourage him to stale (pass water) by whistling quietly.
3. Take off the saddle, rug up the horse, put all the tack and travelling equipment into the tack room.
4. If your horse is dry, remove mud and dried sweat with a body brush. Rub his legs with straw by hand—not with a grooming brush. If your horse is wet, bandage his legs with straw and check his legs carefully for any cuts or thorns which may have pierced his hide. Wrap the straw lightly round the legs and then bandage fairly loosely.
5. Bathe his eyes, nose and dock with a warm, damp sponge.

Pick out his feet and scrub the mud or remaining dirt out of the soles of the feet whilst simultaneously checking the shoes.

6. If the horse is wet from rain, rub over briskly with hay, chamois leather or a stable rubber and use a sweat scraper as necessary. Concentrate on getting his ears and loins dry. Cover the horse's loins with a rug, except when drying that area, to avoid the horse catching a chill. When you have got him as dry as possible put some straw on his back, put his rug on top and then put on the roller. The straw helps to absorb moisture and keeps air circulating under the rug, thus facilitating the drying. Remove rug after twenty minutes and replace with another rug if necessary. If you have no spare rug turn the night rug inside out with straw underneath and keep horse's under-blanket off him until he is dry.

After half an hour, give the horse a fresh bucket of water and feed a bran or linseed mash to him. The mash should have been made when you first arrived home. To make a bran mash, pour boiling water over half a small bucket full of bran and stir until all bran is dampened. Cover with a cloth and leave until cool enough to eat. If feeding linseed it must be boiled, otherwise it may be poisonous.

If the horse breaks out in a sweat at any time up to an hour later it is most likely to be in those areas where he did not sweat in the first place. Dry the ears, throat and loins by using hay and then by rubbing a small area with the heel of the hand in the direction of the horse's coat. Begin where there is a dry area and gradually move out from this area. In addition, if the weather is mild enough lead the horse out. Leave the horse to eat his hay while you clean his tack and the horse-box. Then when you have finished take the horse's rugs off, replace them, remove bandages, give him a feed, water and leave him. Later in the evening go to the stable to check that the horse is comfortable.

The day after hunting

First thing in the morning trot the horse 'in hand' and check for any sign of lameness—he may well be a little stiff in his joints today. Examine again for cuts or thorns. Any over-reaches, that is, wounds on tendons or bulbs of the heels on forelegs where struck by hindfeet, and bruised heels will need treating if not already detected and treated on return from hunting.

Pay attention to your horse's feeding—the excitement of hunting may cause him to go off his feed. Feel his legs for any sign of heat or swelling. If there is, then seek an experienced person's advice; if he is lame or there is excess heat or swelling, call in the veterinary surgeon. Do not work your horse the day after he has been in the hunting field; lead out in hand for about twenty minutes to help wear off any stiffness he may be feeling. If the day is mild he could be turned into his field with a New Zealand rug, which is a waterproof canvas rug, wool-lined with leg straps and a surcingle. Let him graze for about an hour and a half. You may, of course, turn him out each day, not only after hunting.

You may not be an ardent fox-hunting enthusiast but it is well-worth while 'following the hounds', to give a four to five year old horse a light season of hunting. He should go out about once a fortnight for two to three hours at a time, if you want to help him develop that confidence and courage, previously mentioned, before he begins his intensive training as a potential competition horse. If the horse shows real talent as a show-jumper you would not be able to hunt very frequently as well as compete with him because the indoor jumping season of the winter months and the hunting season overlap—it would be asking too much of the horse.

12 Building a simple course

If you have enough space and sufficient equipment, it is a good idea to set up a small course of show-jumps to practise over before competing at a show. Try to build an inviting course with solid-type fences. An example is given below. Some points to note are:

1. Build a free-flowing course with no sharp turns
2. Always use a single pole as the back element in a spread fence
3. Ensure that there are no sharp bolts or spare 'jump cups' sticking out from the jump wings
4. There are four types of obstacle: upright, parallel, staircase and pyramid; try to incorporate them into your course
5. Always begin with a simple spread fence
6. When going downhill horses tend to take a longer stride and vice versa when going uphill
7. Heavy going shortens a horse's stride as does a very restricted area.

Diagram 18

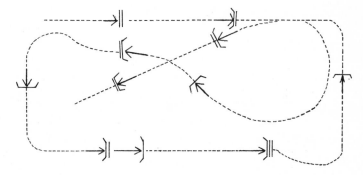

13 Riding a course

The most important preliminary to riding a course successfully is to 'walk the course' thoroughly so that you, the competitor, can envisage it as a whole and in the competition produce a flowing performance from fence to fence.

There are five phases to a jump: approach, take-off, moment of suspension, landing and getaway stride. The rider has four things to consider:— a) determining the horse's track; b) regulating impulsion and speed; c) riding accurate turns and d) avoiding possible refusals.

For the approach, the horse must be in a collected canter and facing the jump in such a way that he can gauge height and spread, while the rider is determining speed of approach. During the horse's strides prior to the take-off, the rider's legs must be firm but ready to move to encourage more energy should he sense any possibility of a refusal on the horse's part.

Rein contact should be light but constant, 'elastic' enough to 'give' as the horse leaves the ground. At the moment of suspension the rider should be looking forward in the direction of travel, seat just clear of the saddle, lower legs encasing the barrel of the horse and the rider already assessing the distance to the next obstacle. As the horse lands, the rider must still be looking towards the next obstacle. It is natural for a horse to lose impulsion coming out of a corner in the course. Many faults occur as a result of badly ridden corners. If the horse does lose thrust in this way he becomes 'flat' in his canter, hollows his back and trails his hindlegs so that as he approaches the jump he fails to gain impulsion and jumps flat, possibly failing to clear the jump, and faults are incurred.

Upright fences may be problematic to the horse but they should not be problematic to the rider. When jumping an upright fence the rider should strive to shorten the horse's stride prior to take-off as he needs to take off at exactly the correct place if he is to clear the fence. Otherwise he will probably get too close to the fence and hit it with his forelegs as he raises his forehand to clear the fence.

When you 'walk the course' before the competition begins, pace out the distance between the combination fences, taking into account the types of fences used. The distances vary slightly according to whether it is a spread to a spread, a spread to an upright, an upright to a spread or an upright to an upright. A difficult combination to be encountered is that which comprises two uprights. For example, a gate to single rails may be used with a distance of 7.25 metres between. If this combination is jumped well it will allow for one non-jumping stride between the two obstacles. The problem is presented by the horse which approaches the first element on a long stride and makes a big and wide jump over it so that he lands too far into the space between the jumps to allow a comfortable stride. Thus he becomes too close to the second jump and then jumps awkwardly in his attempt to get out without knocking down the jump. The rider should bring the horse to such a jump in a short, bouncing stride and make the take-off close to the first element and this will help the horse to jump the second element easily.

When jumping a young horse over his first course of jumps, you should take your time and take from the trot those jumps which you think he will jump better from the trot. Take turns wide so that the horse can maintain good balance. He may well be successful in his first competition and even jump clear all round but the temptation to jump him 'against the clock' should be resisted at this early stage since loss of confidence could result.

14 Fitness of the horse

It is important for your horse to be physically fit and mentally alert. You should establish a regular routine of feeding, mucking out, bedding down and 'strapping' which is the name given to a thorough grooming. Work, when referring to the horse, includes all exercises and activities for the horse in the process of preparing him for what is a specialised sport. Work the young horse for approximately one to one and a half hours a day, excluding his rest day, to keep him healthy and fit, and to prepare him for any competitions in which you want to take part.

When you are actually participating in show-jumping competitions the best form of exercise for the youngster in his fitness programme is walking. This helps to develop all muscles without overstraining the horse. Work at the trot, when it is carried out correctly, helps to develop the strength of all the big muscles of the horse's body and limbs, whilst slow canter work strengthens the horse's stomach muscles and improves his respiration. The ideal way to work your horse is to ride him for up to one and a half hours at the walk and steady trot with an occasional canter. In this way the horse will be using all his muscles to their best advantage without becoming fatigued.

At this point special consideration must be given to the needs of a horse which, as a three-year-old, has been put 'away' to grass until his fourth year and is therefore out of training condition; and those of a recently acquired horse which may have been kept at grass and not ridden objectively and is also in a 'soft' condition must be considered. The process of bringing either horse into peak condition will take as long as eight or ten weeks, depending on his condition when he first comes in and starts his training.

The horse is said to be 'soft' when he tends to fat and has no well-developed muscle and is unable to work for long without sweating a lot and blowing. The horse must be introduced to work gradually. His feed should not include many oats—but mainly hay, properly dampened. Remember to dampen the hay by tipping a bucket of water over the haynet, then hang the haynet outside the stable for about half an hour for the water to drain off.

Trot fences can be used to advantage for the horse who does not use his shoulders. Notice the ground rail at 3 metres to a small spread

A low wide parallel with a pole on the landing side to encourage the horse to use his head and neck

Grooming and care of the feet play an essential part in the fitness programme of your horse

Jumping a 'staircase' fence—the triple bar

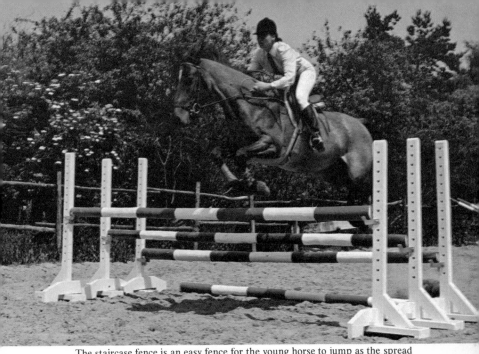

The staircase fence is an easy fence for the young horse to jump as the spread is a gradual one

Jumping a parallel fence. The take-off

Jumping a parallel fence. The period of suspension

A pyramid fence. The landing: notice the even contact with the horse's mouth

The horse will only need about half an hour of walking per day for his first week, after which he can be trotted. As his hay is reduced to about 7-8 kilogrammes, his concentrated food, nuts and oats, should be increased to from 3.5 to 4.5 kilogrammes. In this process of bringing him into good condition, you should make a point of inspecting him each day for any irregularity in his condition, any cut or injury he may have, and any apparent loss of fitness. In a healthy condition the horse should stand alert—head up and ears mobile, pricking back and forth attentively, while his skin should be supple with coat glossy, not 'staring' or with a rough appearance. To take his temperature, shake the thermometer down, grease with vaseline and insert in the horse's rectum keeping hold of the end. Leave for two minutes then withdraw it and read. 38°C is the horse's normal temperature.

The horse should have access to water at all times. Loss of condition can result from an inadequate supply of fresh water.

As a novice-trainer, you will not have specialised knowledge of the medical care of a horse and although I will mention several possible health hazards the wisest course is to seek the advice of a veterinary surgeon whenever you are in any doubt about the horse's condition.

The horse must always be fed the best quality forage. His teeth must be regularly rasped because they do not wear evenly and develop sharp edges. He must also be regularly wormed. A horse can quickly lose condition as a consequence of contracting an illness such as influenza of that contagious catarrhal disease of horses known as 'strangles'. If in any doubt, consult the proper man—the veterinary surgeon.

I cannot stress the importance of gradual training too much. If you try to work your horse too hard too soon after his long rest period, he will soon lose condition. To bring him into hard condition the horse needs sufficient work combined with a carefully balanced diet. In this way fat is turned to muscle, muscles and tendons are toned and the capacity of heart and lungs increased.

15 Preparing for a competition

If your programme to get your horse fit and his schooling have both been successful he should be ready to compete in a show-jumping class after about five months. At this point you should be considering the equipment which the horse and you as rider will need. Also, you have to think of the procedures to be taken by you to enter as a competitor.

The competitor's personal needs include complete riding kit—a hard hat, breeches, boots, white shirt, white tie, black jacket, riding whip, gloves and possibly spurs.

Check your horse's equipment several days before the competition to make sure that it is clean, safe and sound, with special attention to stitching of all pieces.

The horse will need head-collar, rope, grooming kit, summer sheet, anti-sweat rug, roller, poll guard, tail guard, over-reach boots, tail bandage and knee pads; also stable bandages, worn to protect him during his journey to and from the show. As to feed—take a 3.5 kilogrammes net of hay, his usual lunch feed and a water bucket. Water should also be carried in a sealed container since it is not always easily available on the show ground—and when it is located there you will need a container in which to carry it from the source of supply to the horse-box. You will also need his saddle and bridle, a spare girth and pair of reins, a spare pair of stirrup leathers and his studs. Equip the box with a complete first-aid kit for the horse and yourself. Details of these are given on page 89.

During your pre-show inspection you must attend to the horse's shoes. In jumping classes it will be to your advantage to fit the shoes with studs, so be sure that the shoes have screw holes for these when your horse is seen by the farrier well in advance of the show-date. During your preparations, tap out these screw holes and when they are clean, plug them with cotton wool which has been soaked in oil. This ensures that the screw holes can be cleared easily when you need to fit the studs. On the day of the show leave yourself plenty of time so that you are not forced to hurry your horse into the box or trailer and leave home with plenty of time to spare. Try to arrive at the show ground at least an hour before the advertised time of your Class. Both rider and horse should arrive unhurried and calm.

It is important that the novice horse meets a great variety of different obstacles in his early training. The horse and rider jumping a hedge.

16 Travelling

It is essential that, from an early age, a young horse has developed confidence in travelling so that he arrives at his destination without fatigue and nervous tension. To hunt, or compete in show-jumping and other events, you may have to travel considerable distances at times. The business of loading a horse should not be delayed until the day he has to be transported. It is as much a part of his training as any other exercise and it should be well-rehearsed on his home-ground beforehand. It is a good idea to accustom him to his box by loading him and feeding him there, as a part of home routine before actually taking him anywhere. Just as it is advisable to have him take the lead from an older and more experienced horse in other aspects of his training, so here, with his loading into the trailer or box, you can have a more experienced and quiet horse to set a good example by going in first. When he loads easily and calmly, he can be taken for a short journey in the box to get him used to the movement. Here are some hints on loading for the novice-handler.

1. Position the box or trailer by a gate or hedge where a wing will be formed. Place the ramp on an incline so that the angle for entry into the vehicle will be slight. Make sure the interior is not dark by positioning the box in such a way as to get maximum light inside.
2. Let down the ramp at the front but keep the chest bar up.
3. Feed and haynet should be ready. Open all windows and ventilators for more light. You will also need a lunge line or rope and an assistant.
4. Put a head-collar on the horse and a bridle over it. The horse should be fitted with his travelling equipment—tail bandage, stable bandages, knee pads, rug, roller, tail guard, poll guard and over-reach boots.
5. Walk the horse to the box, do not hesitate but do not rush him. Remain close to his shoulder without either looking back or getting in front of him.
6. If you are able to walk the horse inside, have your assistant attach the rear strap promptly to prevent the horse reversing out again the moment you have him inside. Tie him up.

7. After removing the bridle, allow the horse sufficient room to eat his hay but not enough to allow him to turn round or to bite at another horse should there be one in the next partition.

8. In all this seek the help of a person experienced in loading horses.

9. Some horses show reluctance to enter a box. A nervous horse which will not even look at or approach the box is a problem. With this type you must take your time. Never try loading him if you are in a hurry, you will only make him more apprehensive of the box. Handle him calmly and encourage him with a feed; after a while he will probably walk in.

10. The horse which stands at the edge of the ramp and will go no further, swings his quarters and jumps away from the edge, presents another problem. Get the horse to stand quietly as near the ramp as he will, then take a lunge line behind him. Attach one end of a lunge line to the trailer and place the rein behind the horse, gradually applying gentle pressure just above the hocks. Remember to wear gloves, as if he pulls away you may receive a rope burn from the lunge line. Make sure you have an experienced person to help you, as a young horse frightened whilst being loaded will be difficult to box on future occasions. If this does not work, try loading another and less nervous horse first, and perhaps the difficult horse will follow.

11. On any routine day, if you rehearse when no journey is to be made, sometimes feeding the horse in the box, he should not prove difficult when a real need to load him arises.

12. When you are making a journey, the driver should be more than ordinarily careful to give the horse as comfortable a ride as possible, changing gear more frequently than usual to make the going smoother, and driving very slowly, especially on corners, curves and at round-abouts, trying not to give the horse a valid reason for being scared of entering the box in future. A horse which is worried about the loading and subsequent journey will become tense and excited. In such an unsettled state he will not do well in

competitions and if he is to hunt he will become prematurely tired.

On arrival at the place of competition do not unload your horse immediately. First look him over to ensure that he has travelled well. Go to the secretary's tent to collect your number and, whilst there, make sure that you have been entered in the correct class or classes. Locate the collecting ring and scan the map of the course and if you are show-jumping or entered in a cross-country event, be sure that you know the rules of the competition. Walk the course as soon as you can although, if a show-jumping class, this will be just before the competition begins. In the horse-box get the oiled wadding out of the stud holes and fit the studs. The horse should be fitted with studs in each shoe for jumping classes with one fitted at the outside edge of the heel both fore and hind.

Throughout the time at the show let your horse rest as much as possible, by dismounting and slackening his girth. If the day is hot, keep him in the shade—under some convenient tree or on the shaded side of the box—in fact, if your horse loads easily, put him back in his box. This minimises the risk of him being injured in any way, perhaps from the kick of some other rather excited horse, but leave the top doors open so that there is a good circulation of air.

As a competitor in show-jumping you should look to your own appearance, be neatly turned out with your hair tidy.

Before entering you should 'warm up' your horse by mounting and jumping him over a practice fence two or three times. On your entry into the show-ring you may take a preliminary canter round the edge but be sure to wait for the bell before beginning your round—failure to do so will result in your elimination!

When your round is completed, walk the horse about for a few minutes, then load him into his trailer or box and make sure to pat him. Give him some hay and water.

Do not expect to win on your first few outings. The entering of a competition is in itself a valuable experience for both you and your horse. Jumping a round in the strange atmosphere of a show is quite enough for the young horse to experience at this stage. He is not ready to be urged to go round within a time limit 'against the clock'.

17 Training for the rider

The show-jump rider should be an equestrian 'all rounder'. He or she should keep in constant practice, starting with that essential—a deep seat, which makes for harmony of movement between rider and horse. The rider naturally sits in the centre and at the lowest part of the saddle. Sitting squarely, the upper part of the body should be erect and free from any tension, especially in the area of the waist. He should sit upright looking ahead, with the hips vertical to the saddle but without stiffness; the knee and thigh should be in close contact with the saddle, without gripping tightly. Stiffness in the rider's legs will transfer itself to the upper part of the body which will become equally tense. The lower leg should be close to the horse's barrel with the heel below the level of the toes without being forced down unnaturally, in an attempt to achieve 'style'. The back should be firm and upright with the shoulder blades flat; the arms should hang naturally from the shoulders with the elbows bent so that a straight line is formed from the elbow, along the forearm, through the wrist and hand along the rein to the bit. An imaginary vertical line should be drawn from the rider's ear, through the shoulder and hip to the heel.

The stirrup leathers need to be of a length which allows the instep to rest on the horizontal flat of the iron but with a bent knee.

The best way to develop an independent seat is by taking a series of lessons with the horse on the lunge rein which is held by an experienced instructor. Correct riding on the lunge is an excellent way to develop a sympathetic, but deep, seat. With the horse on the lunge line, going on a well-defined circle, the rider has the opportunity to concentrate solely on achieving a good seat, without the normal need to think too much about the control of the horse.

While this is progressing, the instructor has the opportunity to watch the rider's actions and to correct faults in the rider's posture as they become evident. Some instructors will advocate appropriate music to help the rider achieve harmony of movement with the horse—so essential to the skill of the finished equestrian. Lungeing for too long a period at any one time can result in fatigue, soreness and stiffness for the rider who will then become tense and find it difficult to co-ordinate movements properly in a good posture. To avoid this, the rider should start lungeing sessions lasting about twenty minutes, and as he or she becomes accustomed to the exercise and is sitting well, without stiffness, this time can be extneded to about forty-five minutes in each session of training.

Some of this lunge work should be carried out with stirrups but, as the rider becomes fitter and more proficient, most of it should be carried out without stirrups.

Once the rider has acquired an independent seat he can work towards riding for jumping. When jumping, the rider adopts a forward inclining posture. The stirrup leathers should be shortened two or three holes from the length adopted-when riding on the lunge or hacking, so that the angle made by hip and thigh closes—the seat of the rider is therefore made more secure. The rider should be looking forwards in the direction of travel.

The rider's weight should be taken on the stirrup iron by the knee and thigh pressing down towards a deep heel. When riding for jumping, an imaginary vertical line may be drawn from the rider's shoulder through his knee to his toes. In this way, the rider will be able to be in harmony with his horse. The seat must be a mobile one since each jump will involve a canter approach, take-off, suspension, landing and then the get-away strides. This fluid seat and movement of hips free the horse's back, allowing him to jump without feeling the weight of the rider's body on his back; also to recover on landing and get into his stride without undue weight bearing down on his back. The posture also allows the rider's seat to remain just off the saddle, though able to return to it with ease should further control of the horse be required.

Development of the forward inclining posture for show-jumping and the kind of cross-country riding which will involve jumps, can be helped by work over ground rails and cavalletti at the trot.

The rider's hands, with the reins held as for riding on the flat, should be forwards and low, parted one each side of the horse's neck; the straight line from the elbow, along the forearm through the wrist and hand along the rein to the bit, should still be maintained.

Practise the posture by working over ground rails at the rising trot, allowing the upper part of the body to be inclined slightly forwards but with its weight going down into the heels, the knees being firm on the saddle without necessarily gripping. When the horse is settled and going well at trot over the rails, the rider should approach the rails at sitting trot, and continue sitting lightly with the upper body inclined forwards as the horse trots over the poles; on departure from the poles the rider should take rising trot. Throughout these exercises the rider must allow the horse to stretch down and forwards with his head and neck on the approach to, and when trotting over, the poles by giving a little with the hands towards the horse's mouth, whilst still maintaining an elastic contact with the reins.

Supple movement of the loins to gain that deep seat, so necessary for jumping, may be developed by working at the canter. A small grid of fences at a distance of 3 metres apart, so that there is no jumping stride in between, will add to the rider's confidence and improve the stability of his seat. At all stages of approach and jump, the rider's hands should be low and forwards toward the horse's mouth, the body to go with the movement of the horse by bending at hip, knee and ankle, whilst looking ahead.

As the rider gains experience and develops the correct posture and seat for riding both on the flat and over jumps, the enthusiast will want to go over more testing fences. It is important to stress here that the fundamental dressage training must be well learned, since this is just as essential to the show-jumping rider as being able correctly to jump larger and more complicated obstacles.

There is an ideal place, in front of each jump, for the horse to take off; the rider needs to develop an eye for this place and to learn to adjust the horse's stride by lengthening or shortening. A novice rider needs the guidance of a person who has a good eye and who is experienced in training horses to jump. Under expert guidance the potential show-jumping rider will also probably be asked to ride, under controlled conditions—and then later, to jump—without using reins or stirrups. If lessons given are well absorbed, such training will be excellent for attaining true security in the saddle, without depending upon hand or foot for support.

The author schooling a novice horse over parallel telegraph poles at home.

18 Distances

In jumping combination jumps the following scales may be useful to remember as they are likely to be met with in competitions.

Two vertical jumps set at 8.00 metres apart provide one non-jumping stride.

Two vertical jumps set at 11.00 metres apart provide two non-jumping strides.

Two parallels, placed at 7.30 metres apart provide one non-jumping stride.

Two parallels at 10.80 metres apart provide two non-jumping strides.

A vertical jump to a parallel at 7.60 metres apart provides one non-jumping stride.

A vertical jump to a parallel at 10.80 metres apart provides two non-jumping strides.

A vertical jump to a spread at 7.50 metres provides one non-jumping stride.

A vertical jump to a spread at 10.80 metres provides two non-jumping strides.

A parallel to an upright at 7.85 metres provides one non-jumping stride.

A parallel to an upright at 11.00 metres provides two non-jumping strides.

A parallel to a spread (staircase type) at 7.50 metres provides one non-jumping stride.

A parallel to a spread (staircase type) at 10.65 metres provides two non-jumping strides.

A parallel to a spread at 7.30 metres provides one non-jumping stride.

A parallel to a spread at 10.65 metres provides two non-jumping strides.

A spread (staircase type) to an upright at 8.10 metres provides one non-jumping stride.

A spread (staircase type) to an upright at 11.30 metres provides two non-jumping strides.

A spread to an upright at 8.00 metres provides one non-jumping stride.

A spread to an upright at 11.10 metres provides two non-jumping strides.

A spread to a parallel at 7.85 metres provides one non-jumping stride.

A spread to a parallel at 11.00 metres provides two non-jumping strides.

The above distances are measured from the face of the landing side to the face of the take-off side as shown in Diagram 19.

Diagram 19

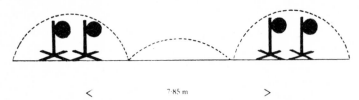

7·85 m

These distances should be regarded as suitable for the horse which stands at about 16 hands. Naturally, the length of individual horse's strides must be assessed to arrive at the best distances for these combination fences—here the length of stride is taken as being one of 3.00 metres. It is, of course, better to practise first with distances which are comfortable for the individual horse and later to progress to more exacting distances by lengthening or shortening them so that the horse learns to be adaptable.

Before competing in a show-jumping class, when walking round the course on foot, take the trouble to pace out distances in the combination jumps so that you will know whether to jump off short or long strides. Upright jumps are best jumped off a short, bouncing stride, but consideration must be given to the distance between jumps in order that the jump 'in' helps to produce the length of stride required to meet the 'out' jump correctly.

Practice over grids is important. When simulating a show-jumping grid, begin with a small fence about 76 centimetres in height. Continue with easily distanced and varied types of fence, increasing height and spread as confidence of both rider and horse is gained.

Footnote   16 hands = 162.7 cms.

19 Faults—and their correction by the trainer

When a horse has, or develops, a fault in his jumping it is essential to find the cause, and then to set about curing the fault.

The horse that rushes his fences, frequently anticipating what is going to be asked of him, is often a tense and nervous horse, and may have carried a rider who 'hung on'—one who lacked depth of seat and confidence and therefore held hard to the reins—or in basic training the horse may have been 'chased'—urged to take fences too large for him too soon in his career and he has been frightened by over-jumping. In such cases the trainer should revert to that basic training which involves walking the horse around fences, over ground rails, then trotting over fences and ground rails, progressing gradually to fences which can be jumped with ease from the canter. Over the ground rails he must be encouraged to stretch his neck downwards towards the ground over which he is travelling. This helps him to arch his back. When he appears at ease with these simple exercises he should be jumped over a few fences at the trot and then returned to schooling on the flat, making several changes of direction, and still including work over the ground rails from time to time.

If this is successful, the horse not trying all the time to anticipate what he is to be asked to do next, jump a simple fence at the canter, pat the horse for taking it in a calm manner and return again to working at the trot over ground rails and small fences and occasionally canter exercises. With such varied and simple work the horse will begin to answer the rider's aids, never anticipating because, with the switch from one simple exercise to another, he will not know what he is to do next and should cease making an impetuous rush at any obstacle.

If a horse is inclined to 'over jump' at a fence, it is a good idea to have a neck strap to reduce the risk of your catching him in the mouth. Each time you approach a fence hold the neck strap as well as the reins.

'Running out' means that a horse has gone past the fence without jumping it. Here again, bad early schooling may be the cause. It may be because the horse was urged to go through exercises too difficult for him too soon. Perhaps the horse has previously been badly positioned for jumps with the approach strides crooked and oblique to an obstacle, or the rider may have been leaning too far forwards, with the seat too far back, thus interfering with the horse's natural pre-jump movements. A horse can show reluctance to jump if the ground surface is hard and jars his joints; equally, if approaches to jumps are slippery he may lose confidence. 'Running out' can of course be just naughtiness or pure disobedience. If a horse has been allowed too much freedom by a previous rider he will be inclined to take such liberties. You, the rider, must be firm, deal with this immediately and make some use of the whip. Decide on the proper angle of approach for a jump and ride the horse to it firmly and with confidence.

If you suspect that the horse is finding a fence too much for him, whatever its size, it is always best to go back a stage in training and not to persist in setting him at the same obstacle. Build a similar obstacle but make it much smaller; align the horse properly for the jump and keep practising at it until the horse jumps it well and thus regains confidence.

In reverting to earlier stages to correct a common fault in a horse which you may have acquired only recently, the progress forward again must be taken slowly with elementary dressage always in mind. Some riders unwittingly make mistakes for which the horse could be blamed, such as losing the contact on the reins at the vital pre-take-off stride. If, indeed, you feel that you are at fault, it is wise to have an experienced rider, unmounted, to watch you and horse in action—that which may appear to you as a fault on the horse's part may in fact be a fault in your riding.

If a horse which hitherto has been jumping well starts to be evasive, you should feel his legs for any heat or swelling; if there are signs of either, call your veterinary surgeon.

At all times you should consult the professional—the veterinary surgeon. The true novice-trainer-owner cannot know what may be wrong with a horse which consistently gives a poor performance. Only regular and thorough physical examinations by the qualified vet can ensure that the horse is fit enough to carry out all that you ask of him. I will only suggest what may be wrong in all my references to health and mention the kind of treatment usually given, but the reader who is in any way uncertain should not hesitate to 'call in the doctor'.

That which applies in very early training—boredom—can apply throughout the horse's show-jumping career. Do not attempt to jump him so intensively and frequently that he becomes bored and therefore jumps and moves slackly and without any apparent zest. Vary his exercises and be selective in any competitions. Do not go for every competition for which you feel yourself and your horse qualified. Compete no more than once a week throughout the jumping season.

If the horse is jumping in a flat or casual fashion the remedy, wise training or retraining apart, is to give him a rest. Turn him out to grass for, say, one month. This also applies if he starts to refuse his fences. If you are keen on hunting, this will provide a suitably vigorous alternative to the more formalised jumping of the show-ring but if hunting is not available or you, as an aspirant to show-jumping, want to concentrate on that sport alone, cross-country riding with a companion on a mature and experienced horse to 'compete' with your own mount, away from the 'school' atmosphere of formal training, will provide a welcome change for your horse and perhaps revive his enthusiasm.

The novice-trainer may find that the horse jumps confidently enough but carelessly, mistiming the take-off point for a fence, either jumping too soon and far from the obstacle or 'getting under' the fence—that is, leaving his take-off too late. In the first instance, he risks taking a fence down with a hind leg; in the second he could put it down with a foreleg. I have found that this can be overcome by a simple arrangement in school or field. The horse can be taught to 'find his way' accurately to a fence by the setting up of a small fence in the centre of the area in such a way that it can be approached and jumped from each side. Try using a figure of eight with the centre of the fence at the middle of the 8.

The fence may be approached from varying angles but always to the centre of the fence. Do not make the angle too difficult to begin with or you may encourage a 'run out'.

In this exercise the horse will learn to judge the moment of take-off and to land in a balanced canter stride.

Some horses tend to jump off their forehand and do not use their shoulders well. This can be corrected by working the horse over trot jumps using short combination distances to low, wide spreads. If you work the horse over a low, wide parallel with ground rail on the landing side at a distance of about 3.50 metres from the rear of the jump, this will encourage the horse to lift his forehand, shoulders and neck and reach out on the departure strides. Such a horse should be schooled 'loose' once or twice during his working week.

The horse which jumps with his back hollow and head too high may have poor conformation. He may have been 'hung on' to by an inexperienced rider or he is maybe impulsive by nature. Such a horse should be worked over a spread fence with a small rail 3.00 metres after the fence, so that the horse is compelled to bring his head down and curve his back as he lands. Another method for eliminating the same fault is to work around a variety of fences, jumping the horse from the trot. In this way he should develop greater thrust from his hindquarters and muscular ability in his back to achieve a good outline in the process of jumping. A series of lungeing exercises would also help to strengthen his back muscles and encourage him to arch his back correctly.

Riding Horse classes are a good way to introduce one's horse to the show ring. Miss Carol Green rides Miss Marie Stokes' horse, Shandover, the Champion Large Riding Horse for the South of England in 1974.

Jumping a pyramid fence

Training the young rider. Jumping a low grid without reins and stirrups

Further grid work for the young rider to improve balance

Jumping a grid with reins and stirrups concentrating on improving the rider's style when jumping

Showing the non-jumping stride between two fences

Studs are essential for the competitive jumper to allow him to jump with confidence

A woollen day rug, which is worn on cold days when travelling

Loading

20 Stable management of show-jumping horses

The following daily routine may be adapted to individual needs in the care of the novice jump or event horse.

07.00 Firstly, inspect the horse to see that he has sustained no injury during the night. Give him fresh water and put on his head-collar and tie up. Clean out the stable and put down the bed. Give him 2 kilogrammes of hay in a hay net. Pick out the horse's feet, fold his rugs back and give him a quick brush over. Sponge his eyes, nose and dock with separate sponges. Feed him. Give him approximately one third of the total daily hard food.

09.30 Remove rugs, saddle up and exercise the horse for up to one and a half hours.

11.00 Untack and water the horse. Tie horse up; pick up any droppings; pick out feet and groom thoroughly, remembering to keep a rug over his back except when you are grooming that area. Put day rugs on the horse. Refill water-bucket, fill haynet with 2.70 kilogrammes of hay. If it is part of your chores, tidy the stable-yard.

12.30 Give horse second feed—1.5 kilogrammes of corn with 0.50 kilogramme of bran and carrots—one third of daily rations.

16.30 Remove all droppings, pick out the horse's feet. Fill up water bucket—remove day rugs and put on night rugs. Clean up equipment then feed 1.50 kilogrammes of corn with 0.50 kilogramme of bran and carrots. Tie up a haynet containing 3.50 kilogrammes of hay.

20.30 Final inspection of stable—check rugs, water bucket and bedding before shutting up the stable for the night.

Horses appreciate a regular routine of exercise and feeding but the timetable which I have suggested may not suit all readers. Whatever your own circumstances, try to set out a routine and adhere to it. The horse will thrive on regularity.

A horse will perform well and benefit by his schooling if his diet is suited to the work required of him. The true novice will, of course, take expert advice on quantities and content, but there are still three salient rules to observe, whatever form the diet takes. (a) Feed little and often. (b) Water the horse before feeding or, better still, leave fresh water always with the horse.

(c) Never work a horse when he has a full stomach. Horses have small stomachs, compared with those of other animals of a comparative size, and a large quantity of water after feeding can cause colic.

By 'little and often' I mean that four feeds a day with plenty of hay in between times helps to relieve any boredom, since this necessitates visits by you to the horse. It should go without saying that you will try to feed your horse the best quality food available.

Remember to feed according to the work the horse is doing. When he is coming into condition after a rest at grass, his diet will consist in the main of bulk food. As his training programme is intensified so, too, should be the degree of concentrated food. If the horse has to stop work for some reason his corn feed should be stopped, and fed bran mashes instead.

Always keep a fresh supply of clean water in the stable, leaving the bucket there day and night, so that the horse becomes accustomed to taking it in short drinks when and as he wants it, instead of drinking in prolonged draughts when it is brought to him.

A healthy horse of 15 to 16 hands would require approximately 13.50 kilogrammes of food a day. This should contain two-thirds bulk—that is, hay and bran—and one-third hard food—oats, barley and horse cubes. When working really hard, the bulk food should be reduced and protein feed increased gradually, according to age and type. Some horses do very well on oats, whereas others can become overheated and thus mischievous and hard to manage so that they need to have a non-heating diet.

The foregoing have been added as general observations on feeding. The wise owner will, of course, consult a knowledgeable horseman about a suitable diet for an individual horse, in terms of quantity and content.

To keep a horse in peak condition he should be groomed daily. Grooming is an essential part of his health programme in that it tones him up—it is not simply for the sake of appearances.

Here is a list of essential grooming tools:

a. Hoof-pick, for cleaning out the horse's feet.

b. Dandy-brush, for removing grease and mud from the

Footnote   15 hands = 152.5 cms. 16 hands = 162.7 cms.

coat—it must not be used on tail or mane. It is a harsh brush and so it must be used gently over the coat of sensitive horses.

c. Body-brush for removing scurf, dried sweat and grease from the horse's coat, mane and tail.

d. Curry comb, to clear and cleanse the body brush.

e. Water brush, to dampen down the mane and tail to make tail hang better and mane to lie flat.

f. Three sponges, one each for cleaning eyes, nose and dock.

g. Mane and tail comb, for trimming and cleaning and removing any tangle or plant segments from a horse which has been at grass. Do not be too forceful when using the comb, the horse's comfort apart, as it is possible to tear the hair.

h. Stable rubber, to give the coat a final polish.

i. Wisp. The wisp, made of straw or, more normally, hay, is used to promote circulation and generally to tone up the horse by massaging his muscular areas.

Your grooming equipment should be kept in a convenient bag or box and when setting about the job you should:

1. Put a head-collar on the horse and tie him up on a short rope with a quick-release knot.

2. Pick out the feet, dropping anything lodged there into a skep or rubbish box for convenient removal, not letting stones and other lumps drop into the stable straw.

3. Use the dandy-brush to remove any dried sweat or caked mud from the body and legs, beginning at the poll on the nearside and working methodically back over the horse, paying special attention to the girth and saddle areas.

4. The body-brush should be used next with the curry comb. On the nearside have the brush in your left hand and the comb in your right hand. Again, start at the poll on the nearside and, working all over the horse, use firm, circular strokes. After every few strokes you should clear the body-brush with the comb. Change hands when grooming the offside.

5. Take the wisp, slightly dampened, and bring it down vigorously over those parts of the horse's body which are hard-muscled—the neck, shoulders, quarters and thighs. This is the 'massage' already mentioned which has the same

toning-up effect on the horse as a trainer's slapping on a boxer's muscles.

6. Take a clean, damp sponge to cleanse the eyes, nose and dock—always in that order. Three separate sponges should be used and immediately cleansed.
7. To 'lay' the mane and tail, dip the end of the water brush into water and dampen—not soak—both.
8. Oil the feet by using a clean paint brush, kept for that purpose alone, and hoof oil. This not only improves the appearance but also has a beneficial effect on the texture of the hoof.
9. Finally, use the stable rubber all over the horse and put on a tail bandage.

It is important for the horse to have a good bed 8 - 10 centimetres deep to encourage him to lie down. Materials used today are wheat straw, sawdust, wood shavings or peat moss.

Straw should be of good quality, seasoned and dry. Short straw is widely used since it is more economical than long and, although the latter is more durable, it is not so easy to handle because of its length. Straw is the best material for bedding the horse since it drains easily and is not difficult to dispose of.

Sawdust must of course be quite dry and in that state is an excellent absorbent, but it will clog up internal stable drains if precautions are not taken to block them before initially introducing the bedding. A fairly heavy metal plate which fits over the drain with a hay wisp underneath will prevent sawdust finding its way into the drain during 'mucking out'. Sawdust is clean and easily handled. Peat moss, another absorbent material, is dark in colour and has certain deodorising properties. It is somewhat heavier to handle than sawdust but it can be used in the same way.

Cleaning out a horse's bed

The method recommended is first, to tie up the horse and remove all surface droppings. Shaking the straw on a fork, start at the door and toss the clean straw to one side of the box. Remove soiled straw in a wheel barrow and sweep the floor clean. Leave the stable to air. When laying down the fresh bed, shake the straw well, bank it up at the sides of the box and leave deep in the middle.

When taking out a sawdust and shavings bed, first remove all surface droppings and rake out any wet patches, then rake from the sides into the middle and lay more sawdust on top.

Bandages

Leg bandages are used to protect the horse's legs, for strengthening and support, for keeping the horse warm and to keep any necessary surgical dressings in place.

Flannel or woollen bandages are used to protect the horse's legs when he is travelling. In the stable they are fitted for warmth. Beginning the rolling-on just below the knee or the hock, continue unrolling clockwise downwards over fetlock and pastern, returning upward to the starting point. Here bandages can be secured by tying the tapes in the middle of the cannon bone, either on the outside or the inside.

Exercise bandages are used for support, expecially if the ground is hard since they absorb shock and counteract the jarring effect on the legs. Once support bandages have been used, the horse will become accustomed to them. He will expect to have them on, and so they will be needed in all jumping exercises and competitions. They are not used for the sake of appearance as some young people seem to think when they have fitted bandages badly on their ponies. If they are not used for their proper purpose they can do more harm than good.

Crêpe bandages are the best and should be put over gamgee, which is cotton wool covered with gauze, starting just below the knee or hock, rolling clockwise down to just above the fetlock joint, and upward again to be secured with the tapes, or stitches, to lessen the possibility of their slipping when the horse is working.

Shoeing

The competition horse should be shod regularly—approximately once a month—in order that the shoes do not wear thin and become loose; also to ensure that the screw holes for studs are not distorted.

A reliable blacksmith is essential for the care of the show-jump horse. The shoe should be made to fit the foot, not the foot trimmed to fit a shoe. The clenches should be even and at the correct height on the foot. The hind shoes should have quarter clips to diminish the chance of an over-reach. The competition horse will require screw holes in the shoes of all four feet at the outside edge of the heels. You should equip your horse with two types of studs. There are dome-shaped studs for hard or medium-hard ground, and square-shaped studs for fitting when the ground is soft. As advised before, when the studs are not in use, the holes should be kept free of any grit and dirt which would become concreted in the holes, by packing the holes with wadded cotton wool soaked in oil. On the day before the competition the holes should be cleared of the old wadding and replaced with fresh, so that on the day of the competition this can easily be removed when you want to screw in the studs. The horse would not, of course, have travelled in his box with his studs fitted because of the risk of injury if he slipped and trod on himself.

Ailments and injuries
Since it is likely that at some time a young horse entered for show-jumping may contract an ailment or suffer some injury, it may be appropriate to give the reader some idea of the health hazards which can sometimes occur. In all cases of doubt, however, call in professional aid—do not, after reading any of that which follows, or anything contained in books on the ailments of horses, try to be your own horse's vet, until you have had years of experience in the care of horses.

When young, every horse should be vaccinated against tetanus and equine influenza. As in the case of all ailments or diseases, prevention of an illness is better than having to find the cure. When a cure is necessary, valuable training time will be lost and the horse will take a long time before being brought back to peak condition.

Tetanus is usually fatal. The disease is caused by the bacilli tetani which enter the blood stream through an open wound, sometimes through very small cuts or abrasions. In the excitement of competing it is easy to overlook small cuts or grazes and that is why I have stressed throughout this book the importance of inspecting your horse, not only at home after his exercises, but also after he has travelled and especially after he has competed. Tetanus is more common in some districts than others. Areas of land which have a high clay content are known to have a higher incidence of the disease.

When a horse contracts tetanus it has a temperature rise to 39.5° or 40.5°C. The membrane of the eye extends over the eyeball and the horse displays nervousness, standing with tail stretched out and head and neck held forwards and down. As the disease takes hold there will be an overall stiffening of the legs, and the jaw will become firmly set; hence the colloquial term for this disease—lockjaw.

Of course the wise owner will call in the veterinary surgeon at the earliest sign of any sort of disorder and if a horse is unfortunate enough to have contracted the disease he will be kept in a darkened box and put on a laxative diet. The vet would advise no hay and ready access to plenty of fresh water.

The most usual type of injury a jumping horse may incur is known as an 'over-reach' or 'brushing' wound, or he may suffer slight injury whilst travelling; hence my advice about leaving plenty of time for the journey and careful driving. Assuming that the horse has indeed been inoculated against tetanus, the treatment of a cut will be much the same as for any small cut and fresh air is the best treatment, provided a wound is clean. No matter how slight the cut, however, the owner should seek out some authority on such an injury. The edges of such a small cut will probably be brought together with gentle pressure and the proper antiseptics applied.

Equine influenza is mentioned, as no matter how well you may care for your horse there are some folk who disregard the risk of passing on this disease by attending gatherings of other horses with their horse which comes from a stable already infected with equine influenza. It is a highly contagious virus infection which can manifest itself in a coughing epidemic among several horses. The horse has a sudden rise in its body temperature which, initially, can reach 39° to 41°C. This high temperature does not, however, last long and for this reason the symptom is overlooked and the contagion can then spread quickly through an entire stable. After the temperature rise the horse will begin coughing, first with a dry and shallow cough which later becomes softer and more fluid. Call in the veterinary surgeon as soon as you can. The cough may last for anything up to fourteen days. The horse will, of course, be taken off work and put on a special diet. Training and exercise can be resumed only very gradually after the coughing has ceased altogether. Acting on the truism that prevention is better than cure, the horse should have an anti-flu injection each year prior to the start of the competition season. Colic is a kind of severe indigestion and one cause is that the horse has eaten too many different types of hay because of excessive travelling away from his home-ground. In the main it is caused by overtaxing the stomach—by the horse being allowed to overeat and usually the wrong kind of food, new oats, mouldy hay, too much boiled food too quickly consumed and not digested properly. A sudden change of normal routine, failure to allow the horse all the water he requires before being fed and working the horse too soon and too hard after its feed, can each result in colic. There are also parasites which cause colic. Excessive quantities of cold water when the horse is overheated is yet another cause.

As soon as you suspect that your horse is suffering from colic you should consult the vet. The symptoms are: the horse will be uneasy, kick at his belly, look round at his flanks, lie down and roll and get up again, and probably start to sweat. The vet will give advice for the early treatment and even if he does not come to the horse straight away, he will at least be standing by. If the advice is to give a colic drench this should always be readily available and should be included in the list of your travelling first-aid equipment—see page 89.

Sick nursing

Whatever advice you receive from the veterinary surgeon, remember that good nursing after his treatment of the horse is very important. After giving prompt attention by calling in the vet as soon as the horse shows unusual symptoms of any kind, the horse should be stabled in a well-ventilated box, free from all draughts, and be isolated as far as possible from other horses in a quiet part of the stables. He will need a clean deep bed of short straw or shavings. Long straw will restrict his movements and tire him if he should want to move around. The loose box should have a half-door but the horse should never be in direct draught or wind although fresh air is important and, again on the vet's advice, he should be allowed to put his head out. If the horse has an injury which necessitates tying him up it is still an advantage to have the top half of the door open so that fresh air will circulate.

Naturally, the horse will have to be kept warm with proper

clothing—rugs and bandages. His box should be cleaned frequently and made fresh at all times. If possible, any medical treatment he receives should be carried out at the same time each day. Part of your nursing will be to keep the horse company. If the horse is very ill he should not be left alone. A sick horse should never be left alone and in the case of serious illness a friend should be available to help you in your watch over him in case of any crisis.

Water should, of course, be changed frequently to prevent it becoming tainted by the ammoniacal fumes of a stable. Do not remove all rugs but just quarter the horse, which is to say fold back the front of the rug and brush the horse lightly; then fold the back part of the rug forwards to brush the quarters. Hand rubbing is comforting to the sick horse and helps to relax him. After any disorder or illness which has meant confinement to the stable, work can only begin on the advice of the veterinary surgeon who will also tell you what form that 'work' or light exercise, may take.

When travelling to horse-shows or a hunt meet, an essential part of your equipment is the first-aid box, or rather boxes, because you should also equip a small box with some simple items for yourself or any companion.

The horse's first aid box should contain—

1. Thermometer
2. Animalintex poultice
3. Wound powder
4. Antiseptic cream
5. Scissors
6. Crêpe bandages
7. Roll of surgical cotton wool
8. Surgical spirits
9. Colic drench
10. Salt—and any other items which your veterinary surgeon may suggest. You will not, I hope, be called upon to give first-aid to your horse but you should have the necessary items ready at hand in the box for a qualified person to do so.

A young horse in a novice show-jumping competition. Notice that the horse is wearing over-reach boots and exercise bandages for the protection of his forelegs.

21 Competitions

If you have been successful enough in training your young horse to bring him 'out' as a well-trained horse, obedient in his paces, with courage and the ability to jump both cross-country and over show-jumps, you will find organised horse trials an attraction and a challenge. Sometimes these are known as 'eventing' competitions.

A good introduction to the sport for both rider and horse may be gained by competing in Riding Club one-day events or, if the competitor is under eighteen, Pony Club events. Many of our more prominent British International three-day event riders began by participating in the Pony Club movement. Pony Club and Riding Club events are of a similar standard. Some riding clubs choose to organise their own horse trials which are usually over a fairly simple course, designed to encourage horse and rider to jump with confidence. The Riding Clubs and Pony Clubs are divided into regions throughout the British Isles. Each region holds its own area horse trials and neighbouring clubs are invited to compete in teams of four over a more taxing course than is normally met with in closed club competitions.

At area horse trials you will encounter a course of show-jumps which will not exceed 107 centimetres in height and a cross-country course with jumps no higher than 1 metre. The dressage tests are of a preliminary standard. The Pony Club has its own tests planned especially for it—these are also of a preliminary standard.

The winning team of the area horse trials will qualify for the National Championships held at Stoneleigh in Warwickshire each year. The championship course is more testing and of a higher standard. Riders and horses successfully completing all three phases of the horse trials at Stoneleigh are, in my opinion, well on their way to competing in the British Horse Society's Official Novice Horse Trials. From success in Novice Trials one would progress to Intermediate, Open Intermediate and finally to Advanced Horse Trials.

British Horse Society's Trials consist of three main tests— dressage, show-jumping and cross-country.

Dressage is a preliminary test lasting about six minutes,

designed to display the standard of a horse's elementary training.

The show-jumping test is taken over a course of eight or ten fences. The courses are normally well-built and include one or two combination fences; in the novice class no fence will exceed 1.14 metres.

Cross-country tests are taken over a course of one and a half to two miles and comprise well-built, solid fences—as many as eighteen in number. This will require a horse of courage with confidence in his rider and the ability to jump solid obstacles at speed; the height in the novice class will not exceed 1.07 metres.

If you are interested in competing in the British Horse Society's Horse Trials you must first register your horse and yourself, as owner, with the Society—address: The British Horse Society, National Equestrian Centre, Stoneleigh, Kenilworth, Warwickshire CV8 2LR. To be eligible, a horse must be 15 hands or over and five or more years old. This is a precaution against the competing of untrained riders attempting to force equally untrained horses to perform under conditions which are far too strenuous for both—the horses lacking maturity and proper bone development. To be eligible the rider must be 16 years old or over so that if an aspirant to show-jumping and cross-country competitions has begun 'eventing' in the Pony Club he or she will be able to progress on to the horse trials as he or she becomes too old for Pony Club activities.

As a competitor, you should learn the rules governing all competitions and these Combined Training Rules, as they are termed, may be obtained on application to the Combined Training Secretary of the British Horse Society. When you are entering do ensure that you are entered in the correct class. At all official events it is necessary to declare formally your intention to compete and you must make certain that your declaration arrives by 12.00 hours on the day before the competition. If you are not able to present yourself in person, then declare your entry by telephone or send a telegram.

You should strive to make it possible for you to walk over the cross-country course on foot the day before the competition. If you have an experienced friend or trainer to accompany you, so

Footnote   15 hands = 152.5 cms.

much the better. If not, do not take a nervous type of person with you—they can influence you adversely. Do not go over the course with a party of people because you may chatter and not concentrate on the reason for being there, which is to assess the jumps, the ground surface and to memorise possible hazards.

Make sure you know the order of each phase. At some competitions the cross-country event takes place before the show-jumping. At other competitions the show-jumping is first. Dressage is always the initial test. It should go without saying that you should yourself be well turned out and not dressed casually. If for no other reason, it is a gesture of respect to the organisers who have worked hard for the success of the occasion and also to members of the public who help to finance it and have paid you the compliment of coming to watch you and your horse perform. Before entering, obtain a copy of the rules where details of dress are given.

The three-day event

To ride in this event is the aim of top-class event riders. The programme is as follows:

1st day—Dressage, a more exacting test than that of the one-day event, lasting about ten minutes. The horse is expected to display obedience and the results of correct training at a more advanced level than that expected of a novice horse.

2nd day—This competition is divided into four phases all of which are timed independently. Phases 'A' and 'C' are endurance tests, the distances totalling between 6 and 10 miles over roads and tracks with the rider using the trot and hand canter as the main paces to achieve an average speed of 240 metres per minute. Phase 'B' is taken over a steeplechase course comprising about twelve fences, not exceeding 1.40 metres in height.

The rider completes this phase at the gallop—speed playing an important part in this test. This phase is ridden at an average speed of 690 metres per minute. On the completion of Phase 'C' there is a compulsory ten minutes pause during which the horse is examined by a veterinary surgeon before being allowed to continue with the next phase.

Phase 'D' is the most taxing part in which the horse is expected to go some 5 miles across country with fixed and solid fences. The successful jumping of these obstacles, as many as thirty in number, will require an experienced rider and horse. The difficulties of each obstacle vary because of differences in terrain in which they are set and the ingenuity of the designer of the course, but they do not exceed 1.20 metres in height.

3rd day—Show-jumping. This is the final day of the competition when the ability of the horse to jump a course of coloured fences, not exceeding 1.20 metres in height, is displayed after two strenuous days of disciplined riding and endurance tests.

Show-jumping competitions are held throughout Great Britain at affiliated shows under the auspices of the British Show-Jumping Association and at purely local competitions which are organised by individual riding clubs, pony club branches, or by private individuals arranging small local shows.

Show-jumping competitions take place over a measured distance in an enclosed arena—usually over level ground. They are designed for the testing of horses from novices to Grade 'A'. The grading is determined by the amount of money the horse has won under British Show-Jumping Association rules. For full details write to the Secretary, British Show-Jumping Association, The National Equestrian Centre, Stoneleigh, Kenilworth, Warwickshire CV8 2LR.

Conversion tables

Use these scales to convert feet and inches into centimetres or millimetres. Convert from feet to metres with the scale on the far right of the page. Convert inches into centimetres or millimetres by comparing the exact measurement on the inch scale with the corresponding measurement on the metric scale. For example, 1 in. equals 2·54 cm. or 25·4 mm. Similarly, 1 ft $1\frac{1}{2}$ in. equals 34·3 cm. (343 mm.).

Convert centimetres or millimetres into inches by comparing the measurement on the metric scale with the corresponding unit on the inch scale. For example, 64 cm. equals 2 ft $1\frac{3}{16}$ in., and 11mm., equals $\frac{7}{16}$ in.

inches	mm.
1in.	1cm.
	2cm.
1in.	3cm.
	4cm.
2in.	5cm.
	6cm.
	7cm.
3in.	8cm.
	9cm.
4in.	10cm.
	11cm.
	12cm.
5in.	13cm.
	14cm.
	15cm.
6in.	16cm.
	17cm.
7in.	18cm.
	19cm.
	20cm.
8in.	21cm.
	22cm.
9in.	23cm.
	24cm.
	25cm.

inches	mm.
10in.	26cm.
	27cm.
11in.	28cm.
	29cm.
	30cm.
12in.	31cm.
	32cm.
1ft 1in.	33cm.
	34cm.
	35cm.
1ft 2in.	36cm.
	37cm.
1ft 3in.	38cm.
	39cm.
	40cm.
1ft 4in.	41cm.
	42cm.
1ft 5in.	43cm.
	44cm.
	45cm.
1ft 6in.	46cm.
	47cm.
1ft 7in.	48cm.
	49cm.
	50cm.

inches	mm.
1ft 8in.	51cm.
	52cm.
	53cm.
1ft 9in.	54cm.
	55cm.
1ft 10in.	56cm.
	57cm.
1ft 11in.	58cm.
	59cm.
	60cm.
2ft	61cm.
	62cm.
2ft 1in.	63cm.
	64cm.
	65cm.
2ft 2in.	66cm.
	67cm.
	68cm.
2ft 3in.	69cm.
	70cm.
2ft 4in.	71cm.
	72cm.
	73cm.
2ft 5in.	74cm.
	75cm.

inches	mm.
2ft 6in.	76cm.
	77cm.
2ft 7in.	78cm.
	79cm.
	80cm.
2ft 8in.	81cm.
	82cm.
	83cm.
2ft 9in.	84cm.
	85cm.
	86cm.
2ft10in.	87cm.
	88cm.
2ft 11in.	89cm.
	90cm.
	91cm.
3ft	92cm.
	93cm.
3ft 1in.	94cm.
	95cm.
	96cm.
3ft 2in.	97cm.
	98cm.
3ft 3in.	99cm.
	100cm.

feet	metres
1ft	30·5cm.
2ft	81·0cm.
3ft	91·4cm.
3ft $3\frac{3}{8}$in.	1 metre (100cm.)
4ft	121·9cm.
5ft	152·4cm.
6ft	182·9cm.
6ft $6\frac{3}{4}$in.	2 metres (200 cm.)
7ft	213·4cm.
8ft	243·8cm.
9ft	274·3cm.
9ft 10$\frac{1}{8}$in.	3 metres (300cm.)

WEIGHT kilogrammes	kg or pounds	pounds
0·45	1	2·21
0·91	2	4·41
1·36	3	6·61
1·81	4	8·82
2·27	5	11·02
2·72	6	13·23
3·18	7	15·43
3·63	8	17·64
4·08	9	19·84
4·54	10	22·05
9·07	20	44·09
13·61	30	66·14
18·14	40	88·19
22·68	50	110·2
27·22	60	132·3
31·75	70	154·3
36·29	80	176·4
40·82	90	198·4
45·36	100	220·5

VOLUME litres	litres or gallons	gallons
4·55	1	0·22
9·09	2	0·44
13·64	3	0·66
18·18	4	0·88
22·73	5	1·10
27·28	6	1·32
31·82	7	1·54
36·37	8	1·76
40·91	9	1·98
45·46	10	2·20
90·92	20	4·40
136·4	30	6·60
181·8	40	8·80
227·3	50	11·00
272·8	60	13·20
318·2	70	15·40
363·7	80	17·60
409·1	90	19·80
454·6	100	22·00

Temperature Conversion

Celsius -18° -10   0   10   20   30   40°

Fahrenheit 0° 10 20 32 40 50 60 70 80 90 100 110°

$C = \frac{5}{9}(F - 32)$ $F = \frac{9}{5}C + 32$